CISTERCIAN FATHERS SERIES: NUMBER NINETEEN

BERNARD OF CLAIRVAUX

TREATISES III

THE WORKS OF BERNARD OF CLAIRVAUX

Volume Seven

On Grace and

In Praise of

CISTERCIAN FATHERS SERIES : NUMBER NINETEEN

TREATISES III

Free Choice

translated by DANIEL O'DONOVAN OSCO
introduction by BERNARD McGINN

the New Knighthood

translated by CONRAD GREENIA OCSO
introduction by R.J. ZWI WERBLOWSKY

CISTERCIAN PUBLICATIONS INC. : *Kalamazoo, Michigan 1977*

These translations are based on the critical Latin edition prepared by Jean Leclercq OSB and H. M. Rochais under the sponsorship of the Order of Cistercians and published by Editiones Cistercienses, Piazza Tempio de Diana, 14, Roma.

Latin titles of the treatises here translated are:
De gratia et libero arbitrio (*On Grace and Free Choice*)
In laude novae militiae (*In Praise of the New Knighthood*)

Ecclesiastical permission to publish this volume was received from Paul V. Donovan, Bishop of Kalamazoo, 19 June 1973.

Library of Congress Catalogue Card Number:
ISBN 0-87907-119-2

Cistercian Publications, Inc.
1749 West Michigan Avenue
Kalamazoo, Michigan 49008

Available in Europe and the Commonwealth from A. R. Mowbray & Co. Ltd., Osney Mead, Oxford OX2 OEG

CONTENTS

ON GRACE AND FREE CHOICE

Introduction by Bernard McGinn 3
Text translated by Daniel O'Donovan OCSO

IN PRAISE OF THE NEW KNIGHTHOOD

Introduction by R. J. Zwi Werblowsky 115
Text translated by M. Conrad Greenia OCSO 125

Select Bibliography 169
Analytic Index

ON GRACE AND FREE CHOICE

INTRODUCTION

WHILE ST BERNARD'S FAME rests primarily upon his reputation as a mystical theologian, as illustrated especially in his *Sermons on the Song of Songs,* it is safe to say that this mystical theory cannot be understood apart from its dogmatic base. Hence the treatise entitled *Grace and Free Choice,* the most profound and influential of the Abbot of Clairvaux's dogmatic works, even in an *a priori* sense occupies a central place in his corpus. Given this importance, i is lamentable that so little attention has been devoted to the treatise-some remarks in E. Gilson's *The Mystical Theology of St. Bernard,*[1] a monograph in Italian by G. Venuta,[2] the thesis of M. Standaert on Bernard's doctrine of the image of God,[3] and a handful of articles are all that the extensive Bernard literature has to show.[4] One previous translation of the treatise into English

1. First published in 1934. English translation by A. H. C. Downes (N.Y., 1940), especially chapter 2.

2. *Libero Arbitrio e Libertà della Grazia nel Pensiero di San Bernardo* (Rome, 1953).

3. *La doctrine de l'image chez Saint Bernard* (Louvain, 1947), *In Sylloge Excerptorum e Dissertationibus,* Vol. 14, fasc. 4. Also published in *Ephemerides Theologicae Lovaniensis,* 23 (1947): 70-129 (this pagination will be followed here).

4. O. Schaffner, "Die 'nobilis Deo creatura' des heiligen Bernhard von Clairvaux," *Geist und Leben,* 23 (1950): 43-57; L. Sartori, "Natura e Grazia nella Dottrina de San Bernardo," *Studia Patavina,* 1 (1954): 41-64; A. Forest, "Das Erlebnis des *Consensus Voluntatis* beim heiligen Bernhard," *Bernhard von Clairvaux, Mönch und Mystiker* (Wiesbaden, 1955): 120-27; E. Kleinedam, *"De triplici libertate.* Anselm von Laon oder Bernhard von Clairvaux? " *Cîteaux,* 11 (1960): 56-62; G. Bavaud, "Les rapports de la grâce et du libre arbitre. Un dialogue entre saint Bernard, saint Thomas d'Aquin et Calvin," *Verbum Caro,* 14 (1960): 328-38; and U. Faust, "Bernhards 'Liber de Gratia et Libero Arbitrio': Bedeutung, Quellen und Einfluss", *Analecta Monastica* 6 (*Studia Anselmiana* 50, Rome, 1962).

exists.[5] No excuse then need be made for a new attempt to assay the significance of the treatise, whatever the judgments to be made regarding the performance. This "Introduction" will not only attempt to isolate the major themes of the treatise but will also strive to present a determination of its place in the deveoopment of the discussion of grace and free will, one of the fundamental question of the history of Christian thought.

THE GENRE OF THE TREATISE

No great difficulties of dating or of textual transmission are presented by the treatise on *Grace and Free Choice*. The work is an early product of Bernard's pen, probably written about the year 1128,[6] and thus a companion piece to such other early treatises as the *Apologia* to William of St Thierry, *The Steps of Humility*, and *On Loving of God*. The recent edition of J. Leclercq and H. Rochais has established a definitive text,[7] the basis for the present translation, and also afforded a discussion of the textual transmission.[8] More important for understanding the work is the determination of the literary genre to which it belongs.

Anselm Le Bail has noted that the mystical theology of the great Cistercian authors presupposes a theory of the soul and its powers. Many Cistercians have left us works explicitly devoted to the soul, Bernard has not. Le Bail and others would see in the *Grace and Free Choice* the equivalent of such a treatise.[9] While the work is among the most important documents for the understanding of the Abbot's theory of

---

5. W. W. Williams, *The Treatise of St. Bernard Concerning Grace and Free Will* (London, 1920).

6. See J. J Leclercq and H. M. Rochais, *Sancti Bernardi Opera*, 9 vols (Rome, 1955-) (Hereafter cited as OB) 3:157.

7. OB 3:165-203.

8. OB 3:157-63.

9. "Saint Bernard," *Dictionnaire de Spiritualité*, Vol. 1, cc. 1461; 1472 (Paris, 1935). See also Schaffner, "Die 'nobilis Deo'" 45; and Venuta, *Libero Arbitrio*, 17, note 1, who notes the qualifications with which this description must be taken.

the soul, and of man in general,[10] neither in form nor in content is it best understood as a *De anima* treatise. Another hint at the genre of the work may bring us nearer the truth. In his discussion of three "blocs" at the basis of Bernard's mysticism, E. Gilson admitted a certain incompleteness in his analysis. "For there is at least a fourth 'bloc' that entered into his patiently constructed edifice. This is the doctrine of liberty contained in the Epistle to the Romans, whence Bernard drew his *De gratia et libero arbitrio.*"[11] The Abbot himself asserts the extent of his dependence on Paul toward the end of the treatise when he proudly claims: "We trust the reader may be pleased to find that we have never strayed far from the Apostle's meaning."[12] While making use of a wide range of Paul's other writings, especially the Epistles to the Corinthians and to the Galatians, it is certainly the Epistle to the Romans which is the major Scriptural basis for the *Grace and Free Choice.*[13]

In one sense, then, the treatise might be said to be Bernard's commentary on Romans. And yet even this does not fully capture its essence. *Grace and Free Choice* is not constructed in the form of a scriptural commentary, either of the traditional patristic-monastic type or of the Scholastic variety then in its infancy. Rather than being controlled by the order of the sacred text itself, the Abbot of Clairvaux fastens his attention on the essential problems of the relation of grace and freedom posed by Romans. The order is his own. Augustine's treatises against the Pelagians and Semi-Pelagians provide the nearest models for the work, and Augustine also gives us a succinct description of its character and aim: "For in this letter of mine [*The Spirit and the Letter*] we have not

---

10. For Bernard's anthropology see W. Hiss, *Die Anthropologie Bernhards von Clairvaux* (Berlin, 1964); and E. von Ivánka, "La structure de l'âme selon Saint Bernard," *Saint Bernard Théologien,* ASOC 9 (1953): 202-08.
11. Gilson, 220, note 23.
12. Gra 14:48.
13. Bernard cites it eighteen times explicitly and twenty-five times implicitly. It should be noted how seldom the abbot engages in allegorical interpretation in a dogmatic treatise of this nature.

undertaken to expound this epistle, but only, mainly on its authority, to demonstrate, so far as we are able, that we are assisted by divine aid toward the achievement of righteousness. . . ."[14]

The key to understanding this central work of Bernard's is to be found in its place in the history of the theological problem of grace and free will. What were the issues involved? What solutions had already been offered and which were influential upon the Abbot? What was the nature of his contribution and what further history was it to have? An adequate answer to all these questions would surely involve the equivalent of a history of Christian theology. Our primary task, of course, is the analysis of the work itself, but this analysis demands some sketch of the background out of which the Abbot wrote.

The problems of the nature of the human will and its relation to freedom are not ones that are peculiar to the history of Christianity. Many of the most important issues involved were already familiar to pagan philosophical traditions.[15] Nevertheless, it cannot be denied that the fundamental tenets of the Christian faith placed the problem of freedom in a central position, and did so by introducing a new series of complications and paradoxes into an already involved area.

As a means of providing some insight into the patristic and medieval evolution of the question, Christian speculation concerning human freedom may be viewed as influenced throughout its history by two complexes of related, but still distinguishable, concerns. The first could be termed the abstract complex, that which deals with the reconciliation of divine foreknowledge and predestination with the contin-

14. *De spiritu et littera* 12:20 (*CSEL* 60:173). Translation from *Nicene and Post-Nicene Fathers*. Series 1, Vol. 5, 91.

15. Two general surveys are V. Bourke, *Will in Western Thought* (N.Y., 1964); and M. Adler, *The Idea of Freedom* (N.Y., 1958-61), 2 Vols. Important for the medieval context is the chapter "Free-Will and Christian Liberty," in E. Gilson, *The Spirit of Mediaeval Philosophy* (N.Y., 1940).

gency of human actions. It explores the implications inherent in the dilemma: either God truly foreknows and infallibly causes all things and hence everything happens necessarily, or at least some human actions happen contingently as the products of free choice and therefore God's knowledge and will are limited. The second complex is concrete and historical, concerned with the relation of man's freedom of choice in the various states of history to sin and to grace. More particularly, granted the fallen state of man, what freedom, if any, does he still retain to choose good or evil? What kind of freedom did Adam have before the Fall? And finally, if justification is entirely the work of God's grace, what kind of freedom remains to the Christian in the state of grace? As Bernard's interlocutor put it in the exchange reported at the beginning of the treatise: "What part do *you* play, then, . . . or what reward or prize do you hope for, if it is all God's work?"[16]

Obsiously, the two sets of concerns influenced each other and were frequently considered together in the course of the same treatises; nevertheless, the history of Western theology shows the usefulness of distinguishing the two. The abstract complex of "providence-predestination-contingency" can be thought of as the more general one upon which the solutions worked out in the complex "sin-grace-freedom." This view, however, presupposes a somewhat speculative notion of theology and a positive attitude to the relation between philosophical and Christian speculation which was on some occasions not present and on others either deliberately rejected or considered unessential. Yet the abstract complex should not be thought of as purely philosophical, no matter how much the complexities of its treatment owe to philosophical systems, particularly that of Aristotle. The Scriptures do speak of providence and predestination as well as of sin and grace, and thus virtually every Christian theology has had to take some stand with regard to certain of the problems involved in what we have called the abstract complex, even if it refuses

16. Gra 1:1.

to consider them in the light of philogophical categories. In short, while our two complexes may very well be thought of after the manner of ideal-types, they have a real heuristic value in helping us to structure the history of Christian speculation on freedom.

The dominance of the concrete schema of sin-grace-freedom during the patristic and early medieval period, as well as a particular cast which it took, is indicated by the very title of Bernard's treatise *De gratia et libero arbitrio, On Grace and Free Choice.* It is important to note that it is the term "free choice" (*liberum arbitrium*) and not "free will" (*libera voluntas*) which is the operative one in Bernard and throughout most of the period in question. The problem was essentially that of man's ability to perform free acts. An explanation of freedom need not be intimately involved with a developed theory of the will; particularly before the period of High Scholasticism medieval authors rarely took up their pens to write treatises *De voluntate.*

One great advantage of the term *liberum arbitrium* was its inclusion of the rational component in freedom. Despite the stress on lack of coercion as the essence of freedom, patristic and medieval authors were never unaware of the delicate problems involved in relating the action of the intellect and the will. Certain High Scholastic writers tried to solve these problems by holding that *liberum arbitrium* was a separate faculty in man, superior to intellect and will.[17] Even in Thomas Aquinas it was not until the *Prima Secundae* of the *Summa* (1269) that the term *liberum arbitrium* lost equal footing with *voluntas* in the systematic analysis of human freedom.[18] Thus it is around the fundamental problems involved in the term *liberum arbitrium* rather than around the systematic concern to elucidate the notion of will that the patristic and medieval approach to the problem developed.

17. For example, Peter of Capua, Geoffrey of Poitiers, and Albert the Great. In this connection see O. Lottin, "Libre arbitre et liberté depuis Saint Anselme jusqu'a la fin du XIIIe siècle," in *Psychologie et morale aux XIIe et XIIIe siècles,* 6 Vols. (Louvain-Gembloux, 1942-1960), 1:219-20.

18. See B. J Lonergan, *Grace and Freedom: Operative Grace in the Thought of Thomas Aquinas* (London-N.Y., 1971), 93.

The theology of Augustine of Hippo provides the *terminus a quo* for the treatment of grace and free choice in the medieval period. Naturally, it is impossible to give any idea of the complex evolution and profundity of his ideas in a brief compass; but in terms of the ideal complexes we have delineated, some broad characterization of his central concerns and influence on the medieval context may be made. First of all, it should be noted that Augustine's attention was largely restricted to the concrete complex of "sin-grace-freedom," partly due to the exigencies of polemic and partly to the philosophical and theological horizon within which he worked. Secondly, Augustine equated the will with the exercise of free choice[19] and provided much impetus for that tradition which discussed grace and freedom primarily under the rubric of *liberum arbitrium* rather than *voluntas*. Finally, he was much concerned, especially in the later stages of his career, with problems of providence and predestination; but in only a few texts was this concern developed within the abstract context of contingency and necessity.[20]

Augustine's views on grace and freedom are polemical, dogmatic, normative, and unfinished. They are polemical insofar as their origin is to be sought not so much in developments out of his own theoretical concerns (e.g., the *De Trinitate*) as in responses he was called upon to make to the challenge of Pelagianism.[21] They are dogmatic in that his primary intent was not so much to seek to understand (insofar as human capability can) the mystery of the divine will and human freedom, but to display the faith of the Church as based upon the Scriptures.[22] Despite the unsystematic and partial

---

19. Bourke, *Will in Western Thought,* 81-2; and E. Gilson, *The Christian Philosophy of St. Augustine* (N.Y., 1967), 157.

20. In the *De civitate Dei* 5:9-10; and the *De libero arbitrio* 3:2-4, Augustine treats the relation between foreknowledge and contingency by introducing the distinction between the kinds of necessity which was to become one of the touchstones of the abstract complex.

21. For a recent survey in English of Augustine's theological response to Pelagianism and Semi-Pelagianism see E. Teselle, *Augustine the Theologian* (N.Y., 1970), Chap. 5:2; and 6:1-2.

22. On the dogmatic character of Augustine's theology of grace, see Lonergan, *Grace and Freedom,* 4-5.

character of his writings, however, their magnitude, insight, and power were to assure them a normative position in the history of Western theology. A medieval theologian might venture to reinterpret Augustine; he would rarely openly disagree with him. Finally, Augustine's thought on grace and freedom was unfinished—at least in the sense that its unsystematic character and polemical cast could easily lead to demands for the harmonization of divergent expressions and inconsistencies, real or imagined. His work was also incomplete in the sense that the speculative thrusts made into the knottiest problems of grace and free choice, to some minds at least, could only be solved by an advance across the board to a new and more systematic level in the treatment of grace and its related problems.

Insofar as the influence of the content of Augustine's views on the medieval development is concerned, several general tenets are of special significance for the path that we will trace.[23] In his writings against the Pelagians and Semi-Pelagians the bishop of Hippo, faithful to his mentor St Paul, made it quite clear that the total initiative in the life of grace rested with God and not with man. So despite the loss of the canons of the Second Synod of Orange (529) during the medieval period,[24] a perspicacious reading of Augustine could always forestall an overly optimistic view of the freedom of fallen man to perform any saving action. But Augustine by no means concluded from this that fallen man had completely lost the capacity of freedom of choice, nor did he assert that some kind of assent was not necessary in the process of justification. Granted the great difficulties of reconciling freedom of choice with the inability to choose the saving good, absolute determinism remained abhorrent to the

23. The literature is vast. Along with the general works already mentioned, H. McSorley in *Luther: Right or Wrong?* (N.Y., 1969), 63-110, contains an analysis of Augustine's major treatises on these questions.

24. See H. Bouillard, *Conversion et grâce chez S. Thomas d'Aquin* (Paris, 1944), 98-102; 114-21.

African Doctor.[25] Furthermore, his attempt of an historical survey of the state of free choice in the various periods of
salvation history was to be a topic of major concern throughout the history of Western theology.

If Augustine is the master of the concrete complex of "sin-
grace-freedom," then Boethius may be taken as the major
influence in the less immediately significant, but eventually
very important, abstract schema of "providence-predestination-contingency." His long discussion of the relation of divine foreknowledge and the possibility of free choice in the
Consolation of Philosophy[26] not only laid stress upon distinguishing varieties of necessity as Augustine had done, but also
stressed the presentiality of God's knowledge as a key to
overcoming the false implications involved in the notion of
foreknowledge.[27] In his second commentary on Aristotle's
On Interpretation, Boethius advanced a definition of free
choice which served to transmit the Peripatetic intellectual
emphasis to medieval authors.[28]

Thus the early twelfth-century context within which Bernard wrote his treatise was open to influences from both the
abstract as well as the concrete complex, though the concrete
question of the historical states of freedom predominated.
We must not think that Early Scholastic speculation on grace
and free choice was nothing more than a repetition of Augustine or a series of footnotes to his treatises. Still, it is true to
say that the theology of grace and freedom of the time was,
in large measure, the first attempts to come to grips with the
speculative problems implicit in the dogmatic heritage of the
Augustinian tradition. Such an immense task could scarcely

25. McSorley, *Luther,* 109-10. The distinction between the freedom left to man
after the fall and the freedom to choose the good is frequently expressed by the
difference between *liberum arbitrium* and *libertas.*

26. Book 4, prosa 6 to the end of Book 5 (Loeb Classical Library, ed. E. Rand,
338-410).

27. Book 5, prosa 6 (ed. 398-410).

28. "Liberum de voluntate iudicium." *In librum Aristotelis de interpretatione
libri sex. Editio secunda,* 3 (PL 64:492-3). On the importance of this definition
see Lottin, *Psychologie et Morale,* 16-7, note 3; and Gilson, *The Spirit of Mediaeval Philosophy,* 310-1.

have been initiated with other than halting steps; the fundamental lines of its development were not to be clarified until
well into the thirteenth century. The careful research of
Artur Landgraf and Odo Lottin among others, as well as the
insights of Bernard Lonergan provide some avenue into this
complex world.[29]

Among the issues of fundamental speculative significance
with which Early Scholastic theology was concerned we may
isolate the definition of free choice (*liberum arbitrium*),[30] the
determination of the various states of liberty, and the nature
of the causal relationship between grace and free choice as
central. While it may be true that the adequate correlation of
these questions was eventually achieved only by the emergence of the notion of the supernatural habit in the thirteenth century,[31] the intellectual energy which twelfth-century authors put into the investigation of these questions is
evidence of the speculative exigence at work in this early
period. These men were by no means content merely to repeat the wisdom of their forefathers. Rather they sought to
achieve a balance between traditional theological authority
and the more systematic demands of their contemporaries.
The variety and invention with which they approached this
task is what gives the early twelfth century its distinctive
flavor.

It is scarcely surprising that the first important treatises on
grace and free choice in Early Scholasticism come from the
pen of Anselm, the Archbishop of Canterbury. Both at the
beginning of his theological career with the well-known treatise *On Freedom of Choice* (c. 1080-85) and toward the end

29. Lottin, *Psychologie et morale au XIIe et XIIIe siècles* (Louvain-Gembloux,
1942-60), 6 Vols.; Landgraf, *Dogmengeschichte der Frühscholastik. Erster Teil.
Die Gnadenlehre* (Regensburg, 1952-53), 2 Vols; and J. Auer, *Die Entwicklung
der Gnadenlehre in der Hochscholastik* (Freiburg, 1951). Lonergan, *Grace and
Freedom*, Chap. 1 gives a synthetic view.

30. Lottin claims that the nature of *liberum arbitrium* was the dominant problem until the middle of the thirteenth century when its place was taken by the
analysis of liberty itself (*Psychologie et Morale*, Vol. 1, 12), though, of course, the
problems cannot really be separated (Vol. 1, 223).

31. Lonergan, 16-9.

with his more mature *On the Harmony of the Foreknowledge, the Predestination and the Grace of God with Free
Choice* (c. 1107-08), Anselm shows his fascination with these
topics. His works are a programatic statement of many of the
issues that were to exercise the wits of a generation of theologians: e.g., the definition of free choice, the explanation of
Adam's freedom to sin and the freedom that remains in fallen
man despite his inability to do good works, and finally, the
determination of how the real freedom (or uprightness, as
Anselm would say) of free will can only be restored by God.
We must not be led to think, however, that Anselm's influence alone was responsible for the dominance of these problems. Wider factors—cultural, educational, and above all theological—were at work in its origin; Anselm's contribution was
characteristically brilliant in isolating the problems, but ques-
tionable in its solutions. His views, especially his definition of
liberum arbitrium from the point of view of final causality, as
the ability to keep uprightness (*rectitudo*) of will for its own
sake,[32] were to have a considerable following; but were never
to be universally accepted. Furthermore, in Anselm's later
treatise it should be noted that the first two parts are devoted
to the abstract problems of foreknowledge, predestination,
and contingency, an innovation that on the whole was not to
be pursued by his immediate successors.

After Anselm's death in 1109, the banner of theological
effort passed to the more conservative theologians associated
with the Cathedral School at Laon, such as William of Champeaux and Anselm of Laon. Our evidence for the teaching of
this School, fragmentary and of subsequent character as it is,
indicates that the Laon theologians were more successful in
appropriating the past than in making significant advances in
the resolution of the problems involved.[33] Such appropria-
tion of the complex heritage of Christian speculation on
grace and free choice was necessary before a new stage could
come into being. There is evidence to indicate that the de-

---

32. *De libertate arbitrii* 3; and *De concordia praescientiae et praedestinationis et
gratia Dei cum libero arbitrio* 1:6 (*Sancti Anselmi Opera*, ed. F. Schmitt, Vol. 1,
212; Vol. 2, 256).
33. Lottin, 15-20.

cade of the 1120's saw such a new stage. The *De sententiis divinae paginae,* dependent on the writings of the Laon theologians and of uncertain date, distinguishes between three definitions of *liberum arbitrium,* that of Anselm, that of Augustine, and that of Boethius:[34] a sign of some maturity in the work of collation and comparison. But the most significant theological work of this decade on these problems was not a work of the Schools, but that of the "Last of the Fathers," Bernard of Clairvaux.[35]

A COMMENTARY ON BERNARD'S TREATISE

The Abbot of Clairvaux addresses the work to his close friend and theological companion, William, the abbot of St Thierry. The two had been friends for a decade or more and William had already produced some of the works which were to make him one of the most profound mystical theologians of the century. Bernard begs suggestions for emendations in this "obscure subject," but we have no idea of knowing how much William himself may have contributed to the process of correction.

Reference has already been made to Bernard's account of the situation which prompted the writing of the treatise. Bernard's questioner was obviously not a Semi-Pelagian: his difficulties appear to have related to the role of free will in the justified man, but the Abbot used the occasion of a query concerning a doctrine of good works and merit for a review in depth of all the ramifications of the connection of grace and freedom.

By way of anticipation, he begins with a brief summary (1:2) of the fundamental relationship between the two: there is a cooperation between grace and free choice, but all the initiative must be ascribed to grace. Nonetheless, the dignity of free choice is already manifest. If no one but God can grant salvation, nothing but free choice can receive it. "To

34. *Ibid.*
35. On Bernard's theological position in 1120's see J. Châtillon, "Influence de Saint Bernard sur la scolastique," *Saint Bernard Théologien,* 275-6.

consent is to be saved," and only free choice, not the natural appetite that man shares with the animals, is capable of this. The voluntary consent of which the Abbot speaks is then defined as "a self-determining habit of the soul," for where the will exists freedom must also be found. This identification of the will with the power of voluntary consent is capped by Bernard's assertion that this is what he means by "free choice."

Right at the outset of his treatise, then, the Abbot of Clairvaux declares his agreement with the tradition that finds in freedom the essence of the will.[36] This is why the remainder of the work will concentrate on the term *liberum arbitrium* rather than *voluntas* itself. Nevertheless, the Saint does wish to provide a firm basis for the understanding of free choice which he advances here. Hence in chapter two he turns to a clarification of the terms involved.[37]

In defining free choice Bernard makes use of none of the three classic definitions of the *De sententiis divinae paginae*: that of Boethius, "the free judgment concerning the will;" that of Augustine, "the power of doing good or evil;" and that of Anselm, "the faculty of preserving uprightness for its own sake."[38] It is a sign of the Abbot's independence of mind that he is ready to provide both his own definition and a framework within which to place it. He distinguishes life, sense-perception, natural appetite, and consent. The consent that he is speaking of here is further clarified as ". . . a spontaneous inclination of the will, or indeed, as I recall expressing it earlier, a self-determining habit of the soul." (2:3). At first glance, Bernard's definition has at least one major misleading aspect, that is the introduction of the term "habit." We must assume that the term is not to be taken in any technical sense, especially not in a strictly Aristotelian one, as

36. Venuta, *Libero Arbitrio*, 59, note 1, notes that Bernard does not even try to prove the existence of *liberum arbitrium* as Augustine had, but presupposes it as an inescapable datum of experience.

37. The most valuable commentary on this section is to be found in Venuta, Chap. 2, "Volontà, Ragione, e Libero Arbitrio," 44-69.

38. Lottin, 16.

Aquinas remarked.[39] In fact, everything that Bernard has to say about *liberum arbitrium* indicates that habit here merely means "a way of acting," and a way that is in no sense infused or acquired, but only expressed, as the actuation of the inamissable nature of man.[40] Consent, as A. Forest pointed out,[41] is not only assent to a particular course of action but the self-actuation of the created spirit—"self-determining" (*liber sui*) is the key term in the definition.

Bernard next turns to an analysis of the relation of will (*voluntas*) and reason (*ratio*) to the essence of consent or free choice. Twelfth-century thinkers were not unacquainted with the delicate problems of the relationship of intellect and will.[42] For the Abbot of Clairvaux will presides over and organizes sense-perception and appetite; but is itself a "rational movement" (*rationalis motus*). Thus, as G. Venuta has pointed out,[43] the two distinguishing characteristics of the Bernardine notion of the will are rationality and liberty. But how does Bernard actually conceive of reason's relation to the activity of the will? Some of Bernard's Scholastic successors interpreted him as holding that the act of judgment was subsequent to the act of the will rather than antecedent.[44] Nevertheless, it does seem that Bernard also admits an antecedent relation, as his emphasis on reason's instruction of the will indicates. There is much about the Abbot's doctrine here (2:3-5) that remains obscure and the subject of disagreement among his interpreters. Reason always accompanies the will, but the will does not always act from reason. "Indeed, it does many things through reason and against reason." This seems to suggest a true and false sense of reason,[45] and perhaps hint

39. *Summa* Ia, q. 83, a. 2, ad 2. Free choice in the Aristotelian sense, of course, is a potency rather than a habit.

40. Venuta, 59-62.

41. "Das Erlebnis," 121.

42. General studies, such as that of Bourke, can be misleading on this point; see his remarks on Bernard in *Will and Western Thought*, 82-3.

43. *Libero Arbitrio*, 48. On Bernard's doctrine of the will see also Hiss, *Die Anthropologie*, 132-7.

44. E.g., Richard Fishacre (died 1248) as cited in Lottin, 116. Bernard's description of reason as the *pedissequa* of *voluntas* probably had much to do with this.

45. Venuta, 55; and W. Williams, *The Treatise*, 8, note 3.

at a notion of an uprightness (*rectitudo*) of reason similar to that found in Anselm. Bernard appears to be saying that some kind of reason must accompany any act of the will, but that good acts of the will will be preceded by correct judgments. Nevertheless, he is true to the traditional Augustinian pattern in continuing to assert that the intellectual judgment cannot exercise necessary causality over the will; otherwise freedom would be an illusion (2:4). The speculative failure, however, is evident, since in neither case, that of good judgment or that of bad, is the nature of the relation really specified. It is not enough to say with G. Venuta that reason exercises some form of indirect action on the will.[46] As perspicacious as Bernard was in identifying the problems, he was no more successful than any other early twelfth-century author in working out the solutions.

A further complication is evident in the ambiguity with which Bernard treats the antecedent and subsequent roles of reason. The consent of the will is what makes man happy or unhappy and thus truly a man, and this consent is once again identified with free choice. "Such consent, I think, is well called free choice, on account of the imperishable freedom of the will and the inevitable judgment of the reason always and everywhere accompanying it, having free disposal of itself because of the will, and power to judge of itself because of the reason" (2:4). But the subsequent judgment which is then discussed is the judgment by which the will judges itself in the act of sinning (i.e. by its failure to be in conformity with eternal truth). Rhetorician to the core, the subtle wordplay between *arbitrium* and *iudicium* in which Bernard indulges in sections four and five of chapter two result in ambiguities of meaning that make it difficult at this juncture to be sure that we have a full grasp of his doctrine of the relation of intellect and will.

Bernard concludes by emphasizing the exclusion of necessity as the fundamental condition of freedom. Only the will in man possesses such freedom, and it alone is the source of

46. Venuta, 56.

merit and judgment (in the subsequent sense). The freedom
that the will possesses is inalienable, it cannot be lost as long
as the will is still a will. Bernard will return to the paradoxes
of this doctrine in the later parts of the treatise. This freedom
is based upon man's possession of rationality, since we can
impute nothing to those who are not masters of their own
reason, such as the mentally deficient, infants, and those who
are sleeping. Thus, the role of reason, even if not still clear in
many respects, is essential to free choice.

Chapter two of the *Grace and Free Choice,* along with the
other passages where Bernard discusses the nature of *liberum
arbitrium,*[47] raises the question of whether the *liberum arbitrium,* is primarily to be ascribed to the will, or to the intellect, or is perhaps to be taken as a separate faculty combining
elements of the other two, as some later Scholastics did. We
know that the status of *liberum arbitrium* was widely dis-
puted during the Scholastic period,[48] and that Bernard was
quoted in support of many opinions. Modern scholars have
continued to disagree on Bernard's views. O. Lottin[49] and A.
LeBail[50] hold that two equal elements, will and reason, are
essential to Bernard's doctrine of *liberum arbitrium*; G. Venuta, after a careful consideration of all the texts, with rather
more justice decides that the consent which is free choice
belongs essentially to the will and that the accompaniment of
the act of reason, while essential, is secondary.[51]

The most influential contribution of the entire treatise is
introduced in the third chapter, the distinction of the three
states of freedom. Due to its inclusion in the *Sentences* of
Peter Lombard, it was to remain a familiar topic of discussion
in the history of Scholasticism. Thomas Aquinas devoted an
article to its defense in his earliest theological work, the *Com-*

47. E.g., 3:6; 4:11; and SC 81:6; OB 2:287-299.
48. Lottin, 11-224.
49. Lottin, 20.
50. Le Bail, c. 1461.
51. Venuta, 62-9, especially 65: "Si potrà cosi anche dire che, entitativamente,
consenso e giudizio sono distinti, per attribuzione d'azione sono la stessa cosa."
He cites Gilson in his support, *The Mystical Theology,* 50-1.

mentary on the Sentences (1252-54),[52] though in his later works he appears not to have found it useful.

The problem that led to the formulation of the states of liberty is an obvious one, and one that shows the dominant position of what we have called the historical complex of "sin-grace-freedom" in the thought of Bernard.[53] The Abbot of Clairvaux may have worked out a definition of free choice that he felt satisfactory, but as a believing Christian how could he square this definition with man's actual state after original sin? If the freedom to choose is so central to human nature that it cannot be compelled from without, how is it that fallen man is not free to choose the good? And does not the intervention of the grace necessary to perform a saving action make a mockery of man's so-called freedom? Are we not compelled by God?

Bernard's answer is to distinguish between various states of freedom. The Abbot's schema is drawn from key texts in the Pauline corpus. There is the freedom that Paul ascribes to the man who possesses the Spirit of the Lord in 2 Cor 3:17, and the "freedom from sorrow" of Rom 8:21. Neither of these can be identified with the freedom discussed in chapter two for which Bernard now coins the term "freedom from necessity," since this best expresses the voluntary character of free choice. The three freedoms are to be identified with the three diverse states of man: freedom from necessity belongs to our natural condition, freedom from sin to the life of grace, and freedom from sorrow to heaven (3:6-7).

The attempt to determine the various states of liberty was not original with Bernard; Augustine among others shows

---

52. *In II Sent.* d. 25, q. 1, a. 5.
53. There is no explicit appearance of the abstract schema in this treatise. McSorley, 134, following R. Mousnier, "St. Bernard and Luther," *American Benedictine Review*, 14 (1963), 460, claims that the Abbot recognized the distinction of types of necessity in SC 81:4—"Ergo quia volens, servam seipsam non modo *fecit*, sed *facit*" (OB 2:289). Bernard may have known of the distinction from its appearance in Anselm, but the very scarcity of its appearance and its lack of development indicate his preference for the concrete schema.

similar efforts. What does seem to be original is Bernard's formulation. In 1940 O. Lottin published a *Sententia de triplici libertate* connected with the School of Laon that was remarkably close to Bernard's position. In his new edition of the text in 1959,[54] he claimed that there was a serious probability that this sentence was authentically from Master Anselm.[55] Since the Laon scholar died in 1117, and since we know Bernard was friendly toward both him and his associate William of Champeaux this would seem to put the Abbot in the position of the borrower. E. Kleinedam, however, pointed out that the close verbal agreement of the texts is actually an argument in favor of Bernard's priority, since his habit is not to quote verbatim but to transform his sources.[56] Furthermore, the triple division does not appear in any of the early *Sentence* collections which can be definitively connected with Anselm,[57] and thus Bernard's origination of the division seems to be vindicated.[58]

In any case, far more important than the origin of the division is what Bernard was to do with it. Specifically, of what dogmatic advantage was it in correlating the teaching of Scripture and the Church on the states of freedom, and of what speculative use was it in explaining how fallen man's inability to choose the good does not destroy his radical liberty? By way of a preview of this analysis (which will occupy the next few chapters), Bernard emphasizes the role of Christ who alone among the sons of Adam possessed all three freedoms and therefore could serve as the liberator of free choice (3:7-8). Christ came to free the will not from necessity but from sin.

Bernard begins the analysis by a deeper exploration of

54. *Psychologie et Morale,* Vol. 5, 87. The text is found in Rouen ms. A. 307(626), f. 220v.

55. *Psychologie,* 82.

56. *"De triplici libertate . . .," Cîteaux* 11 (1960): 60.

57. Ibid., 61.

58. Lottin himself has admitted Bernard's priority in the *Bulletin de théologie ancienne et médiévale,* 8 (1960), #1907; but claimed that the author of the *Sententia* did not copy from the Abbot himself, but from a resumé. Faust, in dependence on the work of J. Leclercq, holds that the *Sententia* does belong to the School of Laon, but is not from Anselm and therefore presumably posterior to Bernard. See "Bernhard's 'Liber de Gratia,' " 41-2.

freedom from necessity. At the beginning of his treatise *On Freedom of Choice,* Anselm of Canterbury had rejected the common definition of free choice as the ability to sin or not to sin since this would make it impossible for either God or the angels to be free.[59] Bernard adopts a similar position here. Just as the saints, angels, Christ, and God possess the fullness of the two final freedoms, so too they have perfect freedom from necessity. Indeed, freedom from necessity is unalterable: "Neither by sin nor by suffering is it lost or lessened; nor is it greater in the just man than in the sinner, nor fuller in the angel than in man" (4:9). The inalienability of free choice defined as the absence of external coercion is once more to the fore.[60]

However, while the essence of free choice remains unaltered, Bernard is willing to make some distinctions regarding the way in which it is possessed. It continues to exist even where the mind is captive to sin. Thus it is full (*plena*) in both good and bad men, but more orderly (*ordinatior*)[61] in the good, and more powerful in the Creator. Here again Bernard seems to show some echo of the Anselmian position on the uprightness of the will;[62] but, as usual, he is transforming his sources.[63]

The freedom from necessity which fallen man enjoys is not freedom from sin. Man's psychological consciousness of his

59. *De lib. arb.* 1 (ed., Vol. 1, 207).

60. The inalienable character of *liberum arbitrium* has led to some discussion concerning the status of the relation between liberty and the soul. After an extensive analysis, Venuta (82-3; 86) decided that *libertas* is a *proprium* of the soul for Bernard, a non-essential characteristic that is nonetheless inseparable. While there is no explicit reason for disagreeing with this position, it should be pointed out: (1) that Bernard displays no interest in such analysis himself; and (2) that Venuta's opinion is based more on SC 80-82 than upon our treatise.

61. The importance of the concept of order in the theology of Bernard has been pointed out by Standaert, "La doctrine de l'image," 71-2; and "Le principe de l'ordination dans la théologie spirituelle de Saint Bernard," *Collectanea Ordinis Cisterciensium Reformatorum,* 8 (1946): 178-216.

62. *De lib. arb.*, especially 3:13-4; and *De concordia* 1:6; and 3:3-4 (ed. Vol. 1, 210-3; 225-6; Vol. 2, 255-7; 265-8).

63. E. Gilson, *La liberté chez Descartes et la theologie* (Paris, 1913), 239-43, compares this passage with Descartes and suggests a source in Gregory of Nyssa.

desire for good and his inability to achieve it indicates that he does have a will (the faculty of desire), and will by definition must be free. He feels that freedom is captive to sin, not that it is lost. Only freedom from necessity, that by which the will can judge itself good or bad is of the essence of free choice. Freedom from sin is better called "free counsel" (*liberum consilium*), and freedom from sorrow "free counsel" (*liberum complacitum*). This new terminology for the triple division manifests the advantage which Bernard hopes to gain for the determination of how fallen man's inability to choose the good does not take away freedom. The key to the validity of the distinction in this area seems to rest on the difference between two intellectual operations, judgment and counsel. Original sin does not take away judgment, the ability to distinguish between right and wrong; counsel, on the other hand, that which determines ". . . the licit as more suitable and . . . the illicit as harmful" (4:11), is denied to fallen man. Neither of these intellectual acts can determine the will, for even the man who possesses grace and *liberum consilium* remains free to sin, but it is the lack of free counsel that is the cause of man's present sinfulness. "Now . . . we discern many things by means of the judgment as either to be done or omitted, which we nevertheless choose or reject through counsel in a manner quite at variance with the rectitude of our judgment (4:11)."[64] Bernard has here offered a clarification of his views on the relation of intellect and will. The antecedent role of intellect is to illuminate the will through a true *judgment,* i.e., one which possesses rectitude, and to show the will what is expedient and licit through free *counsel.* Because this latter is lacking in man since the Fall, he cannot choose the good, and hence the *judgment* subsequently judges his action as evil because of its lack of conformity to truth.

Now the speculative nub of the argument is clear and it is one with which Christian theologians have continued to wres-

---

64. Bernard twice uses the Anselmian phrase *rectitudo iudicii,* here (ed. Vol. 3, 174, line 10) and in 6:17 (178, line 20). See Anselm's treatise *De veritate* 11 (ed. Vol. 1, 191). In 14:49, Bernard speaks of *rectitudo intentionis* (202, line 5).

tle. Granted that the loss of free counsel explains how it is easily possible for man to sin, does it mean that all of unredeemed man's actions are sinful, or is he capable of some actions which fulfill the law even if these are not saving actions? G. Venuta studied this question in the fourth chapter of his *Libero Arbitrio e Libertà della Grazia nel Pensiero di San Bernardo* and affirmed that Bernard, contrary to Augustine, admitted the possibility of virtuous actions among the pagans.[65] However, his position seems unwarranted, for first of all, however much this may seem to be a logical conclusion from what we have just seen, Bernard does not discuss the question explicitly; and secondly, the ability to draw the logical conclusion seems very much dependent on a clear distinction between natural and supernatural virtues that was not available in Bernard's time. Free choice is free for Bernard, but free only to sin.

The triple division of freedom does provide the Abbot of Clairvaux with a definite dogmatic advantage at the end of chapter four. Man's progress from the depths of sin to the glory of heaven is well illuminated by the division. Sunk in sin he possesses only freedom from necessity; he regains, partially but progressively, freedom of counsel through grace, though this cannot be perfectly achieved in this life. Free choice is in captivity to sin to some extent as long as full free counsel is not present. When this is restored in heaven it will be accompanied by the freedom from sorrow that God and the angels enjoy. At the very end of the chapter Bernard introduces an extraneous but typical note by blaming the intellect's weakness at least partially upon its association with the body.[66]

Anthropology

65. Venuta, 103-8; 125-7. Venuta's argument is that the inability of fallen man to fulfill the *whole* natural law affirmed in *De diligendo Deo* 2:6 suggests that he can at least fulfill part of it. But in that passage Bernard seems to be talking more about the impossibility of the total conversion of the will necessary to perform *any* good action. Bavaud, "Les rapports" 337, agrees that the Abbot makes no distinction between the aid that God gives to perform naturally good actions and that which he bestows for supernatural ones.

66. He cites Wis 9:15 in support of this view. The text appears frequently in the treatise, especially in the later chapters; it was also used by a number of other Cistercians, e.g., Isaac of Stella, *Epistola de anima* (PL 194:1875C).

Chapter five briefly examines how far freedom from sorrow and freedom from sin may exist in this world. Freedom from sorrow, or free pleasure, can scarcely be said to be found among men: even virtue does not bring freedom from pain, and the pleasure of vice, false joy that it is, is the most abject sorrow. The pleasure of the goods of the body is unstable, and only the variation between degrees of sorrow may be said to provide some natural joy. True joy is occasionally tasted only in the excess of contemplation,[67] while freedom from sin, or free counsel, is possessed in some degree by all the righteous.

One of the key tensions of the concrete historical complex, that of the relation between sin and freedom reaches its deepest expression in chapter six. Supplementing and deepening positions taken earlier, Bernard fleshes out the concept of the "captivity of free choice" which he mentioned in four. Free choice is captive as long as it is not accompanied by the fullness of the other two freedoms. "To will lies in our power indeed as a result of free choice, but not to carry out what we will" (6:16).[68] In dependence on Paul and Augustine, Bernard now arrives at a deeper explanation of man's inability to achieve good than that manifested by the loss of *liberum consilium*. Not only the intellect, but also the will has been affected by original sin: the will can will, but it cannot will the achievement which is the good; it can only will the bad, the defect that springs from itself. This confirms our conclusion that *liberum arbitrium* alone cannot perform naturally good actions.

But does not such a position effectively destroy real free choice? Bernard, and it must be admitted a number of important Christian theologians from Augustine on, seem to think not.[69] The Abbot says that the essence of freedom is to

67. On the doctrine of *excessus* which Bernard took from Maximus the Confessor, see Gilson, *The Mystical Theology*, 25-8.

68. On the importance of the difference between the will and its efficacy in the Middle Ages see Gilson, *The Spirit of Mediaeval Philosophy*, 316-8.

69. McSorley, 25-9, making use of Adler's survey speaks of three kinds of freedom: natural, circumstantial, and acquired. He claims that what Bernard is speaking of here is only natural freedom, " . . . man's ability to choose and to make decisions" (p. 367), not the power to carry out what he chooses (pp. 133-4).

be affirmed or denied from the point of view of the willing
subject and not from that of the willed object. In other
words, where we have a subject acting spontaneously and free
from external coercion, we have free choice.[70] The eminently
theological character of Bernard's notion of freedom is high-
lighted by the distinction he calls in here to illuminate the
gap between will and performance. Creating grace (*gratia cre-
ans*) is responsible for the existence of the free subject; saving
grace *gratia salvans* for its achievement;[71] or in terms of the
will, from the former we have the simple ability of will, from
the latter the ability to will the good (6:16).[72] Hearkening
back to another notion introduced earlier, Bernard also iden-
tifies the action of saving grace with the "ordering" of the
affections and will given by creating grace.[73] Virtues then are
nothing more than "ordered affections," and it is Christ who
enables us to order them (6:17).

Like Augustine,[74] Bernard goes on to refuse to admit that
free will has perpetual indifference after the Fall. We must
belong either to the devil or to God, i.e., our actions must
spring either from *caritas* or from *cupiditas*. Nonetheless,
when we belong to either God or Satan, we are still our own,

70. As Venuta has pointed out (p. 79) or these two characteristics, one positive and
the other negative, are the essential attributes of freedom for Bernard. The Italian
scholar's summary of the characteristics of liberty on 86-7 is worth noting. The
two fundamental aspects of "non-necessity and spontaneity" and "liberty and
will" result in the "accidentality-inseparability" of liberty's relation to the will.
The final aspect is that of the "universality-integrity" of liberty in thinking subjects.

71. This distinction was fairly popular in the twelfth century; and, although it is
generally Augustinian in character, Bernard's adoption may have had something
to do with its popularity. We find it in a number of authors influenced by him,
e.g., Hugh of St Victor, *De sacramentis* 1, 6:17 (PL 176:273CD); Isaac of Stella,
Sermo 26 in Sexagesima and *Epistola de anima* (PL 194:1774D-75D; 1887D); and
Richard of St Victor, *Liber exceptionum* 2:1 (ed. Châtillon, 114).

72. The formula "Itaque liberum arbitrium nos facit volentes, gratia benevolos"
(ed. 178, lines 3-4) is fundamentally Augustinian, e.g., *Sermo 156* (PL 38:856).

73. P. Delfgaauw, "La nature et les degres de l'amour selon Saint Bernard,"
Saint Bernard Théologien, 235-51, discusses the ordering of the affections. On the
importance of this passage for Bernard's views on *ordinatio*, cf. Standaert, "Le
principe de l'ordination," 188-90.

74. See Teselle, *Augustine the Theologian*, 291-3, for a good summary of
Augustine's refusal to admit complete indifference as the essential note of freedom.

though with the significant difference that when we belong to Satan our own will is the cause, but when we belong to God the cause is his grace (6:18).[75]

The last two sections (19-20) of this important chapter fill out the implications of the prevenience of grace for the other two kinds of freedom that Bernard has distinguished. Perfect willing, i.e., the final stage beyond that of willing the good, needs a twofold gift of grace: true wisdom (*verum sapere*), which is what signifies the conversion of the will to the good, and full power (*plenum posse*), which is the confirmation in the good whose perfection can only be achieved in the next life. True wisdom here is described in terms of the effect it produces on the will; but, as Bernard's language shows, and as he later affirms, it informs the *consilium* of the intellect which enables man to do what is fitting.[76] Free counsel is the freedom to do the good. Conversion is the perfecting good-ness of the will that builds upon the general goodness that it possesses as a part of creation and the special goodness free-dom of choice has as the image of God. For Bernard total conversion, the complete ordering of intellect and will which he has often mentioned,[77] and perfect righteousness are all one and the same; and because they involve the fullness of glory they cannot be ascribed to anyone in this life, not even to Adam, for had he possessed them how could he have sinned?

It is not Bernard's purpose to write a treatise on original sin, but the doctrine of free choice he has expounded and the analysis of the states of freedom he has sketched make it necessary for him to take Adam's original condition into con-

75. Williams, 32, note 1, points to affinities here with Augustine's *De natura et gratia* 23:25 (CSEL 60,251).

76. Compare 4:11 (". . . ita per consilium et *licita,* tamquam *commoda,* nobis *eligere* . . .," ed., 174, lines 2-3) with 6:19 (". . . ut nil *libeat* nisi quod *deceat* vel *liceat,*" 180, lines 10-1). On the equation between *verum sapere* and *liberum consilium* see Venuta, 117-21, who points out how the *sapientia* which Bernard speaks of here is Augustinian in its involvement of intellect and will.

77. 6:19 (ed., 180, lines 19-21) gives an admirable definition of the *ordinatio* of the will: ". . . omnimodo conversio voluntatis ad Deum, et ex tota se voluntaria devotaque subiectio." On total conversion as *ordinatio,* see Standaert, "Le prin-cipe de l'ordination," 202.

sideration. The dilemma in which the Abbot finds himself is
that if Adam possessed only freedom of choice, what did he
lose in being expelled from paradise? If, on the other hand,
he also possessed freedom of counsel and of pleasure, how
did he come to sin? The answer given to this problem is
directly dependent upon St Augustine who in his work *On
Rebuke and Grace* had distinguished between . . . "to be able
not to sin, and not to be able to sin. . . ."[78] Bernard uses this
to show the grades that exist in freedom of counsel and
freedom of pleasure. "The higher freedom of counsel consists
in not being able to sin, the lower in being able not to sin.
Again, the higher freedom of pleasure lies in not being able to
be disturbed, the lower in being able not to be disturbed"
(7:21). The fall of man was a fall into not being able not to
sin and not being able not to be disturbed. This fall took
place through the power of free choice, a power that man
had been given for his glory, but had used for his own condemnation. Man had been given the ability to stand in his
first state; but, since his gifts were only the lower grades of
freedom of counsel and freedom of pleasure, he was not
given the ability to rise again. Free choice, though it remains
free, is now entrapped. The admirable dogmatic precision of
Bernard's triple distinction for the presentation of the Pauline and Augustinian heritage is evident in these succinct and
clear summaries.

The state of not being able not to sin does not put an end
to free choice, it only means that the free counsel by which
man possessed the wisdom and the free pleasure by which he
had the power not to sin have been removed. Free choice is
only responsible for making a creature willing, not for making it wise or powerful. Free choice remains in both the good
and the bad, as long as they possess a will (8:24). The question might occur as to why free choice is not able to regain

78. 12:33 (PL 44:936). Translation from *The Nicene and Post-Nicene Fathers,*
Series 1, Vol 5, 485. On the influence of chapters 11, 12, and 14 of the *De
correptione et gratia* on this chapter of Bernard, see Faust, 44-5. Landgraf, *Dogmengeschichte*, Vol, 1, 102, mentions the discussion of the three states of man
in the *Contra Eutychen* (ed., 122-6) of Boethius as a possible source.

the state that it lost. Bernard, basing himself on the fact that all these states are free gifts of God, shows that it is impossible for man to rise on his own. If Adam before the Fall could not of his own power ascend from the lower to the higher degrees of free counsel and free pleasure, *a fortiori* this is true of our own chance of regaining some measure of these freedoms. Only Christ, "the power of God and the wisdom of God" (1 Cor 1:24), can work the restoration of man's free pleasure and free counsel. Naturally, the perfection of these two, i.e., their higher stages, must wait for the next life.[79] Freedom of counsel enables us not to give way to sin, though we cannot be free of it completely; freedom of pleasure enables us not to fear adversity for the sake of righteousness (8:25-26). The process of learning from free counsel not to abuse free choice in order one day to enjoy full freedom of pleasure is the reparation of the image of God in us (8:27).

Bernard's doctrine of the image of God, outlined in chapter nine, has occasioned much discussion. This is not because the doctrine of the treatise is itself obscure; it is rather that Bernard appears to have held different doctrines at other times.[80] Consequently, the best procedure for the sake of our task seems to be to comment on the position adopted here and then to append a brief discussion of the problems introduced by the other texts.

The image and the likeness of God in which man was created (Gen 1:26) is to be found in the three freedoms. Free choice, because of its unchangeableness has imprinted upon it "some substantial image of the eternal and immutable

---

79. In 5:15, Bernard had held that " . . . on this earth, contemplatives alone can in some way enjoy freedom of pleasure, though only in part . . ." This must refer to the higher freedom of pleasure, if we wish to avoid a contradiction with the present passage which affirms a share in the freedom of pleasure for all the saved here below.

80. For a general approach to the doctrine of the image of God in the twelfth-century theology see S. Otto, *Die Funktion des Bildbegriffes in der Theologie des 12. Jahrhunderts* (*Beiträge zur Geschichte der Philosophie und Theologie des Mittelalters,* 40:1, Münster, 1963); and R. Javelet, *Image et ressemblance au douzième siècle* (Paris, 1967), 2 Vols. For a treatment of Bernard's views, cf. 283-4 in Otto; and Vol. 1, 189-97 in Javelet.

deity."[81] Since free counsel and free pleasure are both subject to diminution or loss they form the accidental likeness
(*similitudo*) of divine power and wisdom (9:28) This observa-
tion concerning the degrees of free counsel and free pleasure
leads the Abbot to introduce a clarification of his earlier
doctrine on the freedoms: instead of the two degrees, e.g.,
"able not to sin" and "not able to sin," we are now given
three, because Adam's ability not to sin was higher and more
perfect than our own, without however attaining to the state
of not being able to sin which God and the angels enjoy
(9:29).[82] Lastly, the Saint turns his attention to the fate of
the freedoms in hell. Scripture itself indicates that both freedom of counsel and freedom of pleasure vanish in hell,
whereas freedom of choice, as has been frequently pointed
out, remains unchanged. Bernard refutes the objection that
souls in hell gain some wisdom from the punishment they
suffer by distinguishing between the sinful act and bad will—
such souls certainly repent of sinful actions, but their evil
wills remain the same.

Chapter ten continues the discussion by summarizing Bernard's doctrine on the restoration of the likeness lost through
sin. Likeness is restored to man and the stain removed from
his image only through the activity of Christ. One note-
worthy point in the allegorical interpretation of the parable
of the woman with the lost coin of Luke's Gospel that he
uses as an illustration here is the introduction of the term
"the region of unlikeness" to describe the state of fallen man.
Since its notice by E. Gilson,[83] the history of this term
(which takes its remote origin in Plato's *Statesman* 273d but
whose major source for the Middle Ages was Augustine's

81. Standaert, "La doctrine de l'image," 76-7, rightly finds some ambiguity in
this doctrine. If what the image consists in is its inalienability and share in the
eternity of God, which comes first? "Le libre arbitre est-il image parce qu'il est
inamissible, ou est-il inamissible, parce qu'il est image?" Both Standaert and Venuta (40) suggest that the latter supposition is more likely.
82. Bernard interprets the scriptural passage "No one born of God commits sin"
(1 Jn 3:19) as proof for the fact that from the point of view of predestination the
sins that the just commit do not interfere with the glory that they shall enjoy
hereafter.
83. *The Mystical Theology*, 45, 115-7, 205, and 223-4.

Confessions 7, 10, 16) has been the subject of extensive examination. Bernard's use probably had much to do with its popularity in the twelfth century, particularly among Cistercians.[84] Christ's position as the "Form" of the Godhead explains how he unites the functions of creator and redeemer. Bernard's lapidary expression could not be bettered: "That very form came, therefore, to which free choice was to be conformed, because in order that it might regain its original form, it had to be reformed from that out of which it had been formed" (10:33).[85] Conformation means that the image should do the same thing in its small world, the body, as the Form, Divine Wisdom, does in the large world of the universe,[86] i.e., it should rule each sense and each member in a way that will prevent sin from reigning. When he is freed from sin, man begins to recover his freedom of counsel and a likeness worthy of the divine image (10:34). Nevertheless, Bernard closes his discussion of man as the image and likeness of God by emphasizing that it is to be understood according to the major lines of the whole treatise. We are not to think that the image, that is, free choice, possesses this power of conformation of itself. This would be to suppose that the essence of free choice rests in the ability to choose good or evil, and Bernard again agrees with Anselm that this view shows its falsity by denying free will to God, the devil, the angels, the saints, and the damned. The Abbot summarily shows once again how free choice as a spontaneous willing free of external coercion must be predicated of God, the devil, and man.

Such is the view of image and likeness found in the *Grace*

84. For a survey of its use in the twelfth century and an introduction to the rich bibliography on the topic see Javelet, *Image et Ressemblance,* Vol. 1, 266-85.

85. On Bernard's doctrine of *forma* here Standaert notes: "Peut-être faut-il dire que *forma* désigne une perfection, ou la perfection d'un être; dans la creature elle est essentiellement participation de la perfection divine, qui crée la perfection finie, et en consitutue l'exemplaire" ("La doctrine de l'image," 118).

86. The text that Bernard used here (Wis 8:1) was later taken up by Isaac of Stella in a similar microcosmic sense in his *Epistola* (PL 194:1885D). On the history of microcosmic themes see R. Allers, "Microcosmos from Anaximandros to Paracelsus," *Traditio,* 2 (1944), 319-409. On microcosmic texts in Bernard, cf. Hiss, *Die Anthropologie,* 72-3, note 16.

and Free Choice. Unfortunately for the neatness of Bernard's doctrine, he could not refrain from discussing image and likeness on a number of other occasions.[87] In the treatise *On Loving God,* probably written slightly before *Grace and Free Choice,* he holds that of the three goods belonging to the soul, (dignity, knowledge, and virtue), it is the first, dignity, which is to be equated with the free choice through which man is said to be made in the image and likeness of God.[88] This rather vague treatment is not unreconcilable with the *Grace and Free Choice,* which still used the word "dignity" to refer to free choice.[89] There are, however, many later texts, some datable and others not, in which quite differing treatments appear. To show their distance from the earlier view it is sufficient to take a look at the most noted, that found in Sermons 80 to 82 of the *Sermons On the Song of Songs* (probably written about 1148).[90] In these Sermons, the soul no longer bears the image of God itself, but is made "to the image" of the true Image who is the Word.[91] This image is said to consist in greatness (*magnitudo*) and uprightness (*rectitudo*).[92] Likeness now is described as threefold, consisting in simplicity, immortality, and free choice.[93] As many have remarked, this leads to an inversion of the view adopted in the earlier treatise, since it is the image now which is lost, at least in part, by sin, and the likeness that is permanent.[94] Bernard himself was conscious of the difference (though perhaps not as conscious as the modern student might have liked), since he closes Sermon 81 with the enig-

87. For Bernard's doctrine of image and likeness, besides the general works, already mentioned, cf. Gilson, *The Mystical Theology,* 46-59; Hiss, *Die Anthropologie,* 66-89; Venuta, 37-43; and especially the excellent survey of Standaert, "La doctrine de l'image."

88. *De Diligendo Deo* 2:2-6 (OB 3:121-124). See Standaert, 74-5. Venuta, 38, claims that in this first Bernardine position free choice equals both image and likeness.

89. E.g., 11:36 (OB 3:191, lines 5-10).

90. On these texts see Standaert, 85-90; and Venuta, 41-3.

91. SC 80:2 (OB 2:277-8).

92. SC 80:5 (OB 2:280-1).

93. SC 81:3 (OB 2:286-8).

94. E.g., Javelet, *Image et ressemblance,* Vol. 1, 195. On 196-7 Javelet notes the influence of William of St Thierry on Bernard's doctrine.

matic statement: "In the treatise which I wrote on *Grace and Free Choice,* are to be read discussions that are perhaps different on the image and likeness, but not, as I think, opposite. You have read those, you have heard these; whichever are to be more favored, I leave to your judgment."[95]

It is not necessary, even were there the space, to survey all the other variations in Bernard's teaching on image and likeness to agree with the judgment of M. Standaert that the Abbot has not one but several doctrines on this question.[96] Nevertheless, there is truth in Bernard's remark about *diversa sed non adversa* if we give the word "doctrine" a somewhat generous meaning, for there is an important common element, a quality of relatedness, in all the things that he had to say about man as God's image and likeness.[97] For our purposes, at least, it is enough to note both the clarity of that aspect of Bernard's views exposed in the *Grace and Free Choice* and its perfect comformability with the rest of the treatise, whatever variations he was to offer at a later time.[98]

Finally, the distinctive character of Bernard's views on man as the image and likeness of God should be emphasized. As E. Gilson has shown,[99] while both Augustine and Bernard place the image of God in man's spiritual nature, Bernards differs

95. SC 81:11 (OB 2:291, lines 13-6). The key phrase in the Latin reads " . . . *diversa* fortassis de imagine et similitudine disputata leguntur, sed, ut arbitror, *non adversa.*"

96. "La doctrine de l'image," 100. In fact, he holds that there are four doctrines in all: those of the formulations of Gra and SC, as well as the irreducible difference between the concept of the soul as the image of the Trinity and that of the soul as the image-imprint (p. 101).

97. Standaert has vindicated this (102-4, 121), finding the common element in the notion of man as *capax Dei,* and the variation at least partially based upon the Scriptural multiplicity of the theme. Hiss, 76-77, also holds for a basic unity, though he bases it upon man's superiority over all other creatures.

98. Javelet, *Image et ressemblance*, Vol. 1, 196-7, speculates that the change in the SC is due to the influence of William of St Thierry. J. Danielou holds that it was the authority of Gregory of Nyssa's *De hominis opificio* to which William drew Bernard's attention that was responsible. Cf. "St. Bernard et les pères grecs," *Saint Bernard Théologien,* 52-5. In this he is followed by M. Canevet, "Gregoire de Nysse," *Dictionnaire de Spiritualité* (Paris, 1967), Vol. 6, c. 1008. Danielou further asserts the possibility of some influence of Gregory on Gra, but admits that the comparisons he draws are very general.

99. *The Spirit of Mediaeval Philosophy,* 210-3.

from his great predecessor in stressing human freedom rather than human intellection as the precise *locus* of the image. The variations in Bernard's own views and the richness of the doctrine in both the Abbot of Clairvaux and the Bishop of Hippo indicate that their views should be seen as complementary rather than opposed, another case of *diversa sed non adversa.*

The eleventh and twelfth chapters form a unit, as do the thirteenth and fourteenth. The first unit revolves around what might be considered difficulties concerning the inalienability of free choice. In this unit chapter eleven serves as a general introduction and chapter twelve considers some classic examples. Neither grace nor temptation take away free choice because God, by sharing his dignity with man, allows the creature to become good (by cooperation with his grace) or evil (through his own fault). God does not take away free will when he converts man, but transfers its allegiance. The Scriptural texts concerning temptation which seem to undermine freedom actually do not touch free choice. Even the captivity to sin of which Paul complains (Rom 7:23) is really the lack of full freedom of counsel, and other Pauline texts are adduced to demonstrate the Apostle's consciousness of his freedom of choice.

Chapter twelve considers the standard objection against the Bernardine theory of will as complete voluntareity, viz., that external coercion is sometimes so strong that free choice seems to be impossible. As befits a theological treatise the example used is a Scriptural one, that of Peter's denial, and in this Bernard seems to express some dependence again on Augustine's *On Rebuke and Grace.*[100] It might be said that those who through fear of death deny their faith either contract no guilt by making a merely verbal denial or are forced to do what they do not will and thus are equally innocent, free choice having perished. Bernard will have none of this: the nature of the will is not such as to admit contrary volitions at the same time. Nonetheless, he recognized the prob-

100. 9:24 (PL 44:931) considers the case of Peter. Faust, 47-8, holds that the dependence is only general.

lem. Peter, for example, did not wish to deny Christ, and therefore it seems that his tongue was moved against his will. What Peter wanted all along was to remain a disciple of Christ's. His will never changed. The objection is put with great rhetorical force, so that Bernard has to try to outdo himself in responding. The key to the answer is given in the objector's admission of two wills in Peter. At first sight, they both appear blameless—the desire to avoid death and joy in being Christ's disciple. However, these are not the two wills that are really in conflict—the real war is expressed in the dilemma "either to lie or to die," and in choosing to lie Peter has preferred the good of the body over that of the soul, an obvious lack to the uprightness of truth in Bernard's hierarchical view of values. The ultimate perduring will in Peter then was not that of remaining a disciple of Christ, as the objector imagined; but in loving himself to excess. The test merely made this free choice evident (12:38).

One might have thought that Bernard had proved his point. Our tastes are not those of the twelfth century, though, and the Abbot's rather long digression on the paradoxes of the "willy-nilly" (12:39-41), however tedious to us, was probably much appreciated by his first readers. To be brief: though it may be true to say that the will is forced, it can be forced by nothing other than itself. Bernard distinguishes two kinds of compulsion, the passive compulsion which can occur without the consent of the sufferer, and the active compulsion which we exert on ourselves.[101] Active compulsion is when the will is prevailed upon to will something which would not happen if we did not will it. Consequently, it is ours and we are responsible for it. In conclusion, the Abbot returns to the fundamentals of his doctrine: free choice, or human will, is located between the divine Spirit and the fleshly appetite. In its present historical state its inclinations are all toward the fleshly appetite; without the assistance of the Spirit it can do nothing. But it is still free.

---

101. See Venuta, 74-5. Interestingly, Bernard gives no examples of varieties of active compulsion nor of passive. One of the real weaknesses in his theory of the will is the great difficulty it has in dealing with questions of mitigated responsibility. A Bernardine manual of casuistry would surely be a slim book.

The final two chapters of the *Grace and Free Choice* concern the relation between the will of God and man's free
decision in the saving act.[102] Here the Abbot returns to the
question posed by his interrogator at the beginning of the
treatise: he thus seems to suggest that only on the basis of a
nuanced doctrine of human freedom can one understand
what part belongs to free choice and what part to grace in the
work of salvation.[103] Bernard's teaching throughout chapter
thirteen is deeply Augustinian. Following his usual practice,
he rarely cites explicitly; but his dependence on Augustine,
especially on the Bishop's own *Grace and Free Choice* treatise is unmistakable.[104]

Making clear that he is not speaking of the special case of
original sin, Bernard reiterates the doctrine with which we
have now become familiar: free choice is either justly condemned because of its own fault, or freely saved through the
mercy of God. The gifts of God are to be divided into merits,
which are our own in the present life, and rewards which
shall be granted to us hereafter. Both, however, have God as
their ultimate source, for "... both our works and his rewards are undoubtedly God's gifts, and he who placed himself in our debt by his gifts, constituted us by our works real
deservers" (13:43).[105] The exact nature of merits, those acts
in which God decides to make use of the ministry of creatures, needs further investigation. Bernard distinguishes three
modes of God's activity upon creatures to specify what he
means by merit. God can act "through the creature yet without it" (*per creaturam sine ipsa*), "through the creature but
against it" (*per creaturam contra ipsam*), or "through the
creature and with it" (*per creaturam cum ipsa*). The first type
of activity pertains to the use that God makes of insensible

---

102. For an outline of Bernard's doctrine in chapters 13 and 14 see Venuta,
chap. 6 "La cooperazione," 137-60.
103. Venuta summarizes: "Ma il suo problema centrale è questo: che cosa fa il
libero arbitrio e che cosa fa la grazia nella salvezza dell'uomo? " (159).
104. The best discussion of the Augustinian sources of the chapter is in Faust,
48-50.
105. Faust compares this with Augustine's *De gratia et libero arbitrio* 21:43 (PL
44:909).

and irrational creatures in his eternal salvific plan; the second
to the way in which he uses evil agents for his own good
purposes.[106] Only the last illustrates the category of merit,
i.e., those activities where God ordains the good will of angels
or men to have the privilege of cooperating with his plan
(13:44). In all three cases we are dealing with instrumental
causes, but only in the third is there a question of merit, as
Paul himself has affirmed. There alone does God's gift of
voluntary consent allow us to say that we are his fellow-workers.

Chapter fourteen follows up this general picture by deter-
mining in greater detail just where the action of grace works
alone and where it deigns to associate human activity with
itself. Again taking his cue from Paul and Augustine, the
Abbot distinguishes three moments in the good act:
". . . thinking, willing, and accomplishing the good; the first
he does without us; the second, with us; and the third,
through us."[107] *Bona cogitatio,* obviously the effective cause
of free counsel, is the realm of purely prevenient grace—
where God acts neither through us nor with us (*nec per
nos . . . , nec nobiscum*). In changing our evil will to consent
to him and giving this consent the ability to perform the
outward action God works without us but through us.[108] Only
the middle stage, however, where he works with us, is that
wherein man can gain merit. An action may give good example, but if it proceeds from some source other than a good
intention, say fear or hypocrisy, it obviously can merit no-

106. Augustine treats of the use that God makes of evil wills in *De gratia et
libero arbitrio,* (PL 44:907) 20:41; and in the *Enchiridion,* 101 (PL 40:279).
Standaert, "Le principe de l'ordination," 197-8, shows the importance of this
threefold use of creatures for Bernard's thought.
107. 14:46. The texts from Paul that Bernard is using here are Phil 2:13; Rom
7:18; and 2 Cor 3:5. While less developed than Bernard, Augustine strikes a
similar note in *De gratia et libero arbitrio,* 17:33: "He operates, therefore, without us, in order that we may will; but when we will, and so will that we may act,
he co-operates with us" (PL 44:901; translation from *The Nicene and Post-Nicene
Fathers,* Series 1, Vol. 5, 458). Venuta, 142-3, note 2, points out that this triple
division differs somewhat from the two given at the very beginning of the treatise.
108. Venuta, 142-9, has a good treatment of Bernard's doctrine concerning
prevenient grace.

thing. *Bona cogitatio* arouses the soul, *bona actio* gives good example, only the *bona intentio* of *consensus* merits. The action of grace upon free choice is described as arousing, healing, strengthening, and saving; in the first case alone is its action prevenient. Bernard goes on to clarify the nature of the cooperation that grace elicits from free choice by stressing that: "It is not as if grace did one half of the work and free choice the other; but each does the whole work, in its own peculiar contribution. Grace does the whole work, and so does free choice—with this one qualification: that whereas the whole is done *in* free choice, so is the whole done *of* grace." (14:47). The admirable clarity of the Abbot of Clairvaux's dogmatic statement of the relation of *gratia cooperans* and free choice has been praised by many.[109] It illustrates both the strengths and the limitations of the treatise: on the one hand, precise doctrinal clarification; on the other, the absence of a speculative explanation of the nature of such cooperation due to Bernard's lack of an evolved notion of the will and theory of causality.[110]

Bernard goes on to show that what he has been describing is nothing other than what the Apostle was speaking of in the famous text from Romans: "So it depends not upon man's will or exertion, but upon God's mercy" (Rom 9:16). Creation, healing or justification, and ultimate salvation (perseverence in grace) are all completely the work of God and not of free will. We ignore God's righteousness if we imagine that our merits proceed from any other source but grace (14:48). Divine action in relation to free choice is threefold: creation, reformation, and consummation. All these are accomplished through the agency of Christ; in all, the divine activity must come first. Only reformation, that which produces the spirit of freedom,[111] involving our voluntary consent, is done with

---

109. E.g., Venuta, 152-3.
110. Faust, 49, also notes Bernard's lack of a doctrine of analogy.
111. For a study of the term *spiritus libertatis* (2 Cor 3:17) in Bernard's writings see A. Dimier, "Pour la fiche *spiritus libertatis*," *Revue du moyen âge latin,* 3 (1947), 56-60.

us (*nobiscum*) and is the source of merit. Bernard has now
established the dogmatic principle at the center of the good
works of the monastic life, and can thus reply to the implica-
tion of his questioner. Good works are valuable since they are
the means by which our inner nature is renewed from day to
day. Again, the Abbot appeals to Paul to show that such
works are both God's gifts in that they come from grace, as
well as our own merits, since they involve consent on our
part. Cooperation alone is the root of merit (14:49-50).

One final problem remains to be clarified. If the will on
which all merit depends is a gift of God (both as will itself by
creation and as good will be reformation), how is it possible
that Paul can speak of a crown of righteousness being laid up
for *him* (2 Tim 4:7)? The answer, of course, is that the
righteousness in question is not Paul's but God's; this righteousness is nothing other than the promise by which God has
freely bound himself to reward those whom he associates
with himself in the work of salvation. The just man, then,
does not trust in his own merits, but in the promise of God, a
note which has been sounded over and over again in the
history of the Christian theology of grace and freedom, not
least of all by the great voices of the Reformation. On this
point the Abbot of Clairvaux ends his treatise.[112]

THE IMPORTANCE OF THE TREATISE IN THE
HISTORY OF CHRISTIAN THOUGHT

It is not our place to attempt a complete evaluation of the
influence that Bernard's *Grace and Free Choice* was to have
on later Christian theology, but some notes concerning this
history will be of help in estimating its significance.

Basic to the historical context in which the Abbot found
himself was the differentiation of the tasks of theology, the
fundamental significance of the development of the Scholastic method.[113] One important part of this differentiation

---

112. For an outline of the system of the treatise see the chart given at the end
of this "Introduction."
113. See B. Lonergan, *Method in Theology* (N.Y., 1972), 138-40.

was the emergence of a clearly-defined and fully-mature speculative moment in the theological operation; this emergence
was something which slowly came to maturity during the
century and a half following Bernard's work. To say that
Bernard's treatise is primarily dogmatic is not to deny him an
important role in this speculative evolution. The Abbot of
Clairvaux was not opposed to Scholasticism as such; his close
association with the theologians of the school of Laon, the
influence that St Anselm exercised upon him, his friendship
with Hugh of St Victor, Peter Lombard, and others, are evidence enough against this.[114] He was merely opposed to what
he rightly or wrongly thought of as aberrations of the use of
reason in theology. Many of the questions which Bernard
discussed in this work were to be central to the development
of later speculation on grace and freedom, especially the definition of free choice, the distinction of various kinds of freedom, and the discussion of operative and cooperative grace
and their relation to merit. Without attempting any detailed
comparisons, it is still instructive to point out some of the
broad lines of this influence. J. Châtillon is undoubtedly correct in claiming that as far as the Scholastics were concerned
the *Grace and Free Choice* was the most influential of all
Bernard's works.[115]

As we have seen, the Abbot's triple distinction of the states
of liberty was apparently almost immediately seized upon as
one of the clearest and most orthodox solutions to a common theological concern. Not only was it copied almost
word-for-word in the *Sententia de triplici libertate,* but it also
appears in the *Summa Sententiarum,* an influential work

---

114. For the abbot's relations with the Scholastics, besides Châtillon, "Influence de S. Bernard sur le scolastique," see also R. Martin, ' La formation théolo-
gique de Saint Bernard," *Saint Bernard et son temps* (Dijon, 1928), 234-40. See
Bernard's EP 410 (PL 182:619A) for his relations with Odo of Lucca and Peter
Lombard.

115. "Influence de Saint Bernard sur le scholastique," 280-1: "Le *De gratia et
libero arbitrio* dont les définitions et les analyses apportaient à la psychologie et à
la morale des doneès vraiment neuves, reste toujours l'ouvrage le plus fréquem-
ment cité et le plus constamment utilisé."

probably written shortly before 1140 by Bernard's friend Bishop Odo of Lucca.[116] Both the *Ysagoge in Theologiam*, a product of the School of Peter Abelard dating from the 1140's and the famous *Libri Sententiarum* of Peter Lombard (c. 1152) make use of the distinction, though they appear to know it through the version found in the *Summa Sententiarum*.[117] Naturally, its appearance in the Lombard's *Sentences* guaranteed it quite an extensive later history, though many authors knew of the distinction directly through Bernard. We also find the triple distinction used by the Abbot's followers in the Order of Cîteaux.[118]

A number of the other topics of the treatise served as direct inspiration for Bernard's contemporaries. Aspects of the discussion of the freedom of man in the face of the loss of free pleasure (11:37-12:40), for instance, were repeated almost word-for-word by Gerhoh of Reichersberg in his *Commentary* on Psalm 31 (c. 1146-47).[119] Other passages influenced the *Commentary* on Psalm 38 written in 1148.[120] Works such as the *Sententia divinitatis* (c. 1145) and the roughly-contemporary *Tractatus de libero arbitrio* of Vivian the Premonstratensian make wide-ranging use of Bernard's work.[121]

Still further, Bernard's strong re-emphasis of the Augustinian tradition, particularly his opposition to Semi-pelagianism under any form, was certainly of real importance, though difficult to trace in its specifically Bernardine form.

The Abbot's contribution to the Scholastic debate on the definition of free choice is capable of more exact determination.[122] Though later Scholastics represented Augustine's

---

116. Controversy still rages over the date and authorship of the work. For the position suggested here, see Lottin, Vol. 1, 25; and J. De Ghellinck, *L'essor de la littérature latine au XIIe siècle* (Paris, 1955), 54-5. On Bernard's influence on the work see also Landgraf, Vol. 1, 88-9; 107; 168.

117. Kleinedam, "De triplicè libertate," 62. Cf. *Libri Sententiarum* II, d. 25.

118. E.g., Adam of Persigny (died 1221), Ep 1 (PL 211:587A).

119. The texts are compared in Faust, 46-7.

120. Leclercq, "Introduction," *Opera*, Vol. 3, 162.

121. Châtillon, 280; and Lottin, Vol. 1, 26-7.

122. The best introduction to the history of the definitions of free choice up to Aquinas may be found in Lottin, Vol. 1, 11-224, especially the summary on 217-24.

view by a definition of freedom of choice as "a faculty of the will and reason,"[123] at the beginning of the Scholastic period the traditional "Augustinian" definition in use was that of "a power of doing good or evil."[124] We have seen Anselm's rejection of this in favor of an essential definition stressing the final cause of freedom—"freedom of choice is the ability to keep uprightness of will for itself alone."[125] Bernard, too, was unsatisfied with the Augustinian definition, but showed his originality by forging his own formula—free choice is a form of consent, i.e., ". . . a spontaneous inclination of the will, or indeed, . . . a self-determining habit of the soul" (2:3). More trenchantly, the Abbot defined it as "freedom from necessity." Some authors have seen an advance in Bernard's definition over that of Anselm, especially in its more adequate treatment of the problem of evil.[126] In any case, Bernard agreed with Anselm more than he differed from him. Liberty defined as freedom from coercion, the complete equation of the voluntary and the free (i.e., that every act of the will as such must be free by definition), and the definition of the soul's justice in terms of its uprightness or "ordination" were all part of the heritage that these two Doctors left to later Scholasticism.[127]

Bernard's definition and its concomitant features became touchstones, frequently cited and commented upon. Hugh of St Victor in his *De sacramentis* (c. 1135-40) also defined free choice through spontaneity, though direct evidence of the

123. William of Auxerre (died 1220) was the first to attribute this definition to Augustine. It actually first is found in Peter Lombard, cf. Lottin, Vol. 1, 64, note 2.

124. This definition was derived from a passage in the *De correptione et gratia*, 1:2: "Liberum itaque arbitrium et ad malum et ad bonum faciendum confitendum est nos habere" (PL 44:917).

125. " . . . libertas arbitrii est potestas servandi rectitudinem voluntatis propter ipsam rectitudinem" *De lib. arbit.* 3 (ed., Vol. 1, 212; translation of J. Hopkins and H. Richardson, *Anselm of Canterbury: Truth, Freedom, and Evil,* N.Y. 1967).

126. Venuta, 164; and Faust, 42-3.

127. On Anselm's influence on Bernard see Gilson, *The Mystical Theology,* 226, note 52.

Abbot's influence is lacking. The *Summa sententiarum*, as might be expected, had a strongly Bernardine doctrine of the relation of will and reason in *liberum arbitrium*.[128] Both Peter Lombard and Richard of St Victor discussed the inadmissability of free choice under the Bernardine rubric of *libertas a necessitate*.[129] In short, the influence of Bernard on his immediate context was extensive.

The Abbot of Clairvaux's importance by no means dwindled in the thirteenth century, for even though theories of the will as an intellectual appetite based on St John Damascene's *De fide orthodoxa* and newly-translated Aristotelian works were becoming increasingly important, the Scholastic mentality always sought to correlate and conciliate its doctrinal authorities. Philip, the Chancellor of the University of Paris (died 1236), was particularly important in popularizing the views of both Anselm and Bernard among later Scholastics.[130] He tried to conciliate the Abbot's claim that free choice was a habit with the enigmatic claim of Peter Lombard that it was a faculty or power;[131] thus creating an unstable position that was bound to be overcome. With two of the most important early masters of the Mendicant orders, the Franciscan Alexander of Hales (died 1245) and the Dominican Albert the Great (active in Paris c. 1243-47), we find that Bernard's definition has become one of four classic positions to be treated in discussing free choice.[132] As the Orders continued to develop and harden their theological traditions during the course of the century, it became obvious that the influence of the Abbot of Clairvaux was more welcome among the Franciscans than among the Dominicans, some-

128. Lottin, Vol. 1, 25-6.
129. Landgraf, Vol. 1, 103.
130. Lottin, 70, note 2.
131. Ibid., 72-6.
132. In Albert the definitions are those of Anselm, Bernard, one attributed to St Peter and the Lombard's version of an "Augustinian" definition (Lottin, 120). With Alexander the four are Anselmian, Bernardine, "Augustine," and philosophical (135-6; 143). This formulation becomes standard in Franciscan authors, e.g., Odo Rigaud (160), and St Bonaventure, *In II Sent.* d. 25, q. 6, 608 (179-80).

thing that held for a dogmatic treatise like the *Grace and Free Choice*, as well as for Bernard's more mystical writings.[133]

Although the influence of Bernard was less marked among the Dominicans,[134] it was not totally absent. Scholars have long discussed the nature of the relation of the Abbot's thought to that of Thomas Aquinas, the master of Dominican theology and the *Doctor communis* of the Catholic Church. While avoiding the extreme of attempting to interpret Bernard in the light of Aquinas, as has been done frequently in the past, or of admitting with Châtillon that Aquinas admired Bernard's virtues more than his theology,[135] there still is value in comparing the two, if only to illustrate whatever lines of continuity may have bound together the vast transformation of Western theology in the more than one hundred years between their writings.

The earliest major work of Aquinas, the *Commentary on the Sentences,* displays a great concern with some of the elements of Bernard's thought which had become part of the theological tradition. As already noted, Aquinas defends Bernard's threefold distinction of liberty and even seems influenced by his definition of free choice.[136] In the first part of the *Summa, liberum arbitrium* remains a topic for treatment, and so does the definition;[137] but the latter parts of this work illustrate that Aquinas' mature thought had less and less place for the *liberum arbitrium* on which the Bernardine treatise is based. Does this indicate complete rejection of Bernard's positions? Perhaps not.

Even if Bernard's formulations were sometimes rejected or superceded, this in no way detracts from their significance; it merely shows that like all theological effort they partake of time at least as much as of eternity. The Abbot's definition of free choice was based upon the equation of the free and

133. Châtillon, 281-3.
134. Ibid., 283.
135. Ibid., 284.
136. *In II Sent.* d. 25, q. 1, a. 1, ad 1.
137. Ia, q. 83, a. 2, ad 2.

the voluntary; Thomas Aquinas had evolved a theory of the will in which all actions of the will were voluntary, but not all were free.[138] The distinction of the various historical stages of freedom, while never totally abandoned because of theology's ties to the history of salvation, yielded pride of place in High Scholasticism to the systematic theorem of the supernatural.[139] The Augustinian terms of operative and cooperative grace continued to be used, but took on more technical meanings within the ambit of a systematic theology influenced by a developed theory of the will as an intellectual appetite, the theorem of the supernatural, and a more nuanced understandings of modes of causality.

For all these reasons, Bernard and Thomas may easily be contrasted in many particulars—and not only in the areas mentioned. What is obvious is the dominance of the abstract "predestination-contingency-freedom" schema in the thought of Aquinas.[140] Nevertheless, as G. Venuta has noted well, Bernard's main concern was not the speculative question of how to reconcile grace and free choice; but the dogmatic problem of presenting the Scriptural and ecclesial doctrine of the roles of free choice and grace in the work of salvation.[141] His goal was fundamentally the same as that of Augustine: to penetrate to the heart of Paul's message on grace. His method was also a very similar one—basically that of the comparison, collation, and exegesis of the Scriptural texts. Obscure texts were illuminated by more manifest ones; distinctions (for the most part suggested by the Scriptures themselves) were introduced to handle key problems; pertinent passages were invoked to guide the procedure. Bernard had not been unwilling to go beyond a purely Biblical theology in such areas as working out a definition of free choice; but the purpose behind such forays was always controlled by the overwhelming dogmatic interest of his treatise—that the teaching of the

138. See Lonergan, *Grace and Freedom*, 93-7.

139. Ibid., 18.

140. For one summary of the agreement and difference between the two see the article of Bavaud referred to at the beginning of this Introduction.

141. Venuta, 159.

Church on grace and free choice should shine forth. It is on
this level, i.e., insofar as both Bernard and Thomas attempted
to be true in their own ways to the fundamental doctrinal
tradition of the medieval Church, that we must look for the
real agreement between them. Agreement did exist on many
important issues: the continuity of some form of freedom
after the Fall, coupled with the radical impotence of this
freedom to effect a saving act; the absolute prevenience of
grace, and the totality of its efficacy; and the admission that
through the activity of grace the will can cooperate in the
work of its salvation, so that free choice becomes the *locus* of
merit. In this sense, at least, the comparison between Bernard
and Thomas does show lines of continuity, although their
respective visions of the nature of theology and the resources
which it should invoke were diverse. Perhaps both Bernard
and Aquinas might have thought of this as a case of *diversa
sed non adversa.*

One final area of the influence of the *Grace and Free
Choice* of the Abbot of Clairvaux deserves mention. It is
common knowledge that among medieval authors Bernard
stood second to none in the admiration of the Reformers.
Given the central position of grace and justification in the
theology of the Reformation, the question of the attitude
taken by this tradition to the Abbot's treatise is a suggestive
one. Since it would be impossible to give an adequate survey
of the whole, we will limit ourselves here to a brief evaluation
of the attitude of Luther and Calvin toward the *Grace and
Free Choice.*

Despite the research that has already been devoted to the
topic, the full complexity of Luther's relation to the Abbot
of Clairvaux invites further study.[142] It does seem fair to say
that after St Augustine, Bernard was Luther's most admired
theologian. "I regard him as the most pious of all monks,"

. Among older studies H. Strohl, *L'evolution religieuse de Luther jusqu'en
1515* (Strasbourg, 1922), especially 107-8, might be mentioned. Two recent, but
on the whole unsatisfactory, treatments in English are R. Mousnier, "St Bernard
and Martin Luther," *American Benedictine Review,* 14 (1963): 448-62; and C.
Volz, "Martin Luther's Attitude toward Bernard of Clairvaux," *Studies in Medieval Cistercian History,* CS 13 (Spencer, 1971), 186-204.

said Luther, "and prefer him to all others, even to St Dominic. He is the only one worthy of the name 'Father Bernard' and of being studied diligently."[143] Or again, "St Bernard was a man so lofty in spirit that I almost venture to set him above all other celebrated teachers both ancient and modern."[144] Nevertheless, Luther made it quite clear that there were important limitations to the esteem in which he held the Abbot. Not only the universal principle by which any author was to be followed only insofar as he adhered to the Scriptures,[145] but a more special principle qualified Bernard's position. Luther says: "Bernard was superior to all the Doctors in the Church when he preached, but he became quite a different man in his disputations, for then he attributed too much to law and to free will."[146] It seems obvious, then, that Luther thought that there was an essential difference between Bernard the preacher and Bernard the dogmatician, and that his admiration for the former did not extend to the latter.[147] The reason for this is not hard to see. While Luther always praised Bernard's emphasis on personal faith in Christ as essential for justification,[148] there were many aspects of the Abbot's teaching on grace and free choice which could

143. *Sermons on the Gospel of John,* 33, in *Luther's Works. American Edition,* Vol. 22:388 (hereafter referred to as AE).

144. *To the Councilmen of Germany* (AE 45:363). For other statements of Luther lauding Bernard see Mousnier, 450.

145. Texts to illustrate the application of this principle to Bernard will be found in Volz, 194-5, and 200-1.

146. *Table Talk* #584 (AE 54:105). Similar remarks may be found in the *Commentary on Psalm 117* (AE 14:38); and *Table Talk* #5439a (not translated in AE, but can be found in the critical edition of Luther's works, the *Weimerer Ausgabe, Tischreden,* Vol. 5, 154). This text contains an explicit reference to the *Grace and Free Choice*: "For Bernard, nothing is worthwhile but Jesus; in his debates, for example the one about free will, Jesus is nowhere to be found." One is permitted to wonder if Luther really knew the treatise well, or if he was merely using his customary exaggeration.

147. Mousnier, 451-2.

148. W. Pauck, "General Introduction," *Luther: Lectures on Romans* (Library of Christian Classics, Philadelphia, 1961), p. I. One example taken from these *Lectures* would be the commentary on 8:16-8, which quotes Bernard's *First Sermon on the Annunciation* (OB 5:234); further texts are collected in Volz, 188-9; 198.

scarcely have been to his liking. The Reformer's great work, *On the Bondage of the Will,* penned in response to the challenge of Erasmus, makes this clear. H. McSorley has pointed out that the fact that Luther rejected freedom of choice in this work did not mean a complete denial of liberty to fallen man;[149] but it cannot be denied that Luther's views on the relation of grace and the human will would naturally have led him to take a jaundiced view of a number of the tenets of the *Grace and Free Choice,* such as its doctrine of good works and merits, and its defense of the permanence of free choice in fallen man.[150] Though Luther's major difficulties with traditional orthodox (i.e. non-Semi-pelagian) formulae may come from his denial of the two kinds of necessity which medieval authors utilized to solve the problems of what we have called the abstract complex,[151] even on the level of the concrete complex of "sin-grace-freedom" the distance between him and Bernard is a real one.

Nonetheless, this should not blind us to the areas of doctrinal agreement that do not exist, particularly those on the impotence of fallen man and the prevenience and efficacy of grace which both authors inherited from Augustine.[152] There are also some texts where Luther's explicit denials may mask at least partial agreement.[153] Of course, Luther's dis-

---

149. *Luther,* 246-50; 256-60; 310-13; 369. Luther's denial of freedom of choice is directed against the definition of Erasmus that is based upon the un-Bernardine liberty of indifference. This is why we can assert that although things happen necessarily they do not happen compulsorily. See *On the Bondage of the Will* (*Library of Christian Classics,* Vol 17, 139-41).

150. Many Catholic authors, e.g., Stutz, 50-1; and Gilson, *The Mystical Theology,* 223-4, note 33, have been quick to point out the differences.

151. Even here McSorley attempts to show that Luther's explicit denial involved an implicit acceptance (315-20).

152. In earlier works, particularly the *Lectures on Romans,* Luther may have been at times basing himself directly on the *De gratia et libero arbitrio,* e.g., his remarks about conformity to the Word (6:16-7, trans. Pauck, 188) may be dependent on Gra 10:33.

153. E.g., in denying the cooperation of the will in the work of man's recreation (*On the Bondage of the Will,* Library of Christian Classics trans., 289), Luther obviously distances himself from Bernard (Gra 14:46). Luther does, however, admit some kind of cooperation even in this passage: "But he [God] does not work in us without us, because it is for this very thing that he has recreated and preserves us, that he might work in us and we might cooperate with him." In

tinction between Bernard the preacher and Bernard the disputant is a false one—there is no essential difference in the positions the Abbot held in the two kinds of works.[154] But what led the reformer to make the differentiation? Was it a question of selective acquaintance, unconscious mental censorship,[155] or what? Again, the anomalies await further investigation.

The relation of Bernard's treatise to John Calvin's theology is less ambiguous than its connection with Luther.[156] Calvin's penchant for scholarship and his precision have much to account for this. Nevertheless, we are still lacking a satisfactory evaluation of all the substantive issues. Forty-seven passages from the Abbot's writings are cited in Calvin's *Institutes of the Christian Religion*;[157] and his extensive knowledge of the treatise on *Grace and Free Choice* is amply illustrated. Insofar as direct citations from the treatise are involved, Calvin mentions Bernard's definition of free will in his discussion of the question (*Institutes* 2, 2, 4), though he apparently holds it lacking due to its obscurity. The Geneva reformer's reaction to Bernard's three states of freedom seems to be conditioned by his knowledge of the history of the distinction in Scholastic theology. In 2, 2, 5, he accepts the distinction ". . . except in so far as necessary is falsely confused with compulsion;"[158] while in 2, 3, 5 he apparently holds that Bernard himself did not fall into this pitfall while Peter Lombard did.[159] He might well have added that many of the Scholastics who made use of the distinction also affirmed a

Bernard's categories of "thinking, willing, and accomplishing," it seems that Luther would admit cooperation in the case of the third, but not in the case of the second.

154. As pointed out by Mousnier, 458-9.

155. Ibid., 460.

156. E.g., See Bavaud for a general survey.

157. See Index II under "Bernard of Clairvaux" in *Institutes of the Christian Religion,* translated by F. Battles and edited by J. McNeill (Library of Christian Classics, Vols. 20-1, Philadelphia, 1960), Vol. 2, 1601.

158. Ibid., Vol. 1, 262.

159. The passage praises Bernard's Augustinian dictum (Gra 6:16) that free choice makes us willers and grace willers of the good. It includes a lengthy quotation from SC 81:7. This dictum of the Abbot is again commended in 2, 5, 14; and the SC passage is also cited in 2, 5, 1.

difference between necessity and compulsion. Calvin, however, also criticizes some positions Bernard had adopted in
the *Grace and Free Choice*. In 1, 15, 3, he rejects any doctrine of man as the image of God which makes use of the
un-Biblical attempt to distinguish between image and likeness; while in 2, 2, 6, he explicitly condemns Bernard's doctrine of operating and cooperating grace.[160] All in all, though,
Calvin's attitude towards Bernard is a remarkably positive
one. In 2, 3, 12, he praises his understanding of the prevenient character of grace,[161] and in 3, 11, 22 couples Bernard
with Augustine in recognizing that men are made righteous
by the free acceptance of God. Most interestingly, in 3, 12, 2,
Calvin even seems willing to accept the doctrine of merit that
he found in the Abbot of Clairvaux. As we have seen at the
end of *Grace and Free Choice,* man's fundamental ground for
confidence is not in his own merits but in the promise by
which God has freely bound himself, a promise made visible
in Jesus Christ.[162] Calvin is willing to concentrate on this
aspect of Bernard's teaching and excuse others—"the fact
that he uses the term 'merits' freely for good works, we must
excuse as the custom of the time."[163]

Thus we can see that Bernard's *Grace and Free Choice,* the
most mature dogmatic product of his pen, did not lose its
influence in the new theological world of the Reformation.

160. There seems to be some confusion about what text of Bernard that Calvin
may have had in mind here, since the Abbot speaks of operating and cooperating
grace in Gra 14:47 and not 14:46, as the editors of the *Library of Christian
Classics* suggest. The point that Calvin is making against Bernard does not, however, apply to 14:47. Calvin says: "Thus Bernard declares the good will is God's
work, yet concedes to man that of his own impluse he seeks this sort of good
will" (ed., Vol. 1, 263); but for Bernard the good counsel which seeks the good
will is always sown by divine activity. The Abbot does, of course, differ from the
reformer insofar as he could be included under the latter's second heading of false
views on the nature of cooperating grace, those who think that we " . . . confirm
it by obediently following it."

161. Citing SC 21:9.

162. The texts that Calvin refers to here are not from Gra 14:51, but from *In
Qui inhabitat* 15:5; and SC 13:4; 61:3; 68:6. The basic doctrine does not differ,
however, though the Christological dimension is stronger in the passages cited.

163. *Institutes,* ed. McNeill, 758. Other passages in which Calvin praises Bernard's understanding of merits are 3, 12, 8 (using SC 13:5); and 3, 15, 2 (citing
SC 68:6).

Just as in the Scholastic context, it was widely read, sometimes followed as authoritative and sometimes criticized. Like all great works of theology, *Grace and Free Choice* is at once intensely time-bound—the product of one man working in the light of a certain dogmatic tradition with a limited number of resources at his disposal—and yet in some way perhaps timeless. The timelessness of theological masterpieces is itself a theological question of no small dimension. Reading Bernard may not provide answers to current theological problems, but it may enable the modern reader to experience something of the elusive transcendence of all true theological classics.

Bernard McGinn

The University of Chicago

PROLOGUE

WITH GOD'S HELP, in so far as I could, I have brought to a conclusion this work on grace and free choice which I recently began on an occasion know to you.[1] I fear nevertheless that I may be found to have spoken less worthily than I might have of these great matters, or to have repeated unnecessarily what has already been treated of by others.[2] You please read it first, therefore, and if you think best, privately; lest, if it be read for the first time in public, it may perhaps advertise the author's temerity more than edify the reader's charity. Then, should you judge it useful to be read publicly, if you notice something obscurely stated which, in an obscure subject, might yet have been more clearly expressed, without departing from due brevity, do not hesitate either to amend it yourself or else to return it to me for emendation, unless you wish to be deprived of that promise of Wisdom where it says: "Those who explain me will have life everlasting."[3]

---

1. In the Latin the second person plural is employed throughout the Prologue.
2. For example, St Augustine, Prosper of Acquitaine, Hilary of Arles and Faustus of Riez, Fathers of the Second Council of Orange (AD 529), and St Anselm.
3. Sir 24:31 (Vulgate).

51

CHAPTER ONE

FOR THE MERIT OF A GOOD WORK THERE IS NEEDED, ALONG WITH THE GRACE OF GOD, THE CONSENT OF FREE CHOICE.[1]

ONCE, IN CONVERSATION, I happened to refer to my experience of God's grace, how I recognized myself as being impelled to good by its prevenient action, felt myself being borne along by it, and helped, with its help, to find perfection. "What part do *you* play, then," asked a bystander, "or what reward or prize do you hope for, if it is all God's work? " "What do you think yourself? " I replied. "Glorify God,"[2] said he, "who freely went before you, aroused and set you moving; and then live a worthy life to prove your gratitude for kindnesses received and your suitability for receiving more." "That is sound advice," I observed, "if only you could give me the means to carry it out. Indeed, it is easier to know what one ought to do than to do it; for it is one thing to lead the blind and another thing to provide a vehicle for the weary. Not every guide supplies the traveller with the food for the journey. The one who sets him in the right direction gives him one thing, the one who provides him with food to keep him from fainting on the way, another.[3] So, too, not every teacher is automatically a communicator of the good he teaches. Hence, I stand in need of two things: instruction and help. You, man, certainly give fine instruction to my ignorance; but, unless the Apostle be

1. The chap. titles are adopted, with some slight modifications, from Watkin Williams, tr. (London: SPCK, 1920), as these seem clear and helpful. They are derived from Mabillon.
2. Jn 9:24.
3. Mt 15:32.

mistaken, the Spirit helps our weakness.[4] Indeed, the One
who advises me by means of your words, must assist me also
through his Spirit, so that I may be able to do as you advise.
For it already is due partly to this assistance that I can will
what is right, but I cannot do it;[5] but I would have no
grounds for believing that I would some day manage to do it,
were it not that he who has given me to will, shall also enable
me to accomplish on account of my good will."[6] — "Where,
then," said he, "are our merits, or where our hope?" —
"Listen," I replied, "He saved us, not because of deeds done
by us in righteousness, but in virtue of his own mercy.[7]
What? Did you imagine that you create your own merits,[8]
that you can be saved by your own righteousness, who cannot even say 'Jesus is Lord' without the Holy Spirit?[9] Or
have you forgotten the words: 'Without me you can do nothing,'[10] and, 'It depends not upon man's will or exertion,
but upon God's mercy'?"[11]

  2. Maybe you are saying: "What part, then, does free
choice play?" I shall answer you in one word: it is saved.
Take away free choice and there is nothing to be saved. Take
away grace and there is no means of saving. Without the two
combined, this work cannot be done: the one as operative
principle, the other as object toward which, or in which, it is
accomplished. God is the author of salvation, the free willing
faculty merely capable of receiving it. None but God can give
it, nothing but free choice receive it. What, therefore, is given
by God alone and to free choice alone, can no more happen
without the recipient's consent than without the bestower's
grace. Consequently, free choice is said to co-operate with
operating grace in its act of consent, or, in other words, in its

  4. Rom 8:26.
  5. Rom 7:18.
  6. See Phil 2:13.
  7. Tit 3:5.
  8. Cf. chapter 13 below; also SC 68:6, OB 2:200.
  9. 1 Cor 12:3.
10. Jn 15:5.
11. Rom 9:16.

process of being saved.[12] For, to consent is to be saved. That is why the animal spirit does not receive this salvation: it lacks the power of voluntary consent, by which it might tranquilly submit to a saving God, whether by acquiescing in his commands, or by believing his promises, or by giving thanks for his benefits.

VOLUNTARY CONSENT IS ONE THING, NATURAL APPETITE ANOTHER [13]

For voluntary consent is one thing, natural appetite another. The latter we hold in common with irrational animals.[14] Ensnared by the allurements of the flesh, it has not the power of giving consent to the spirit.[15] Perhaps it is this the Apostle is referring to under another name as "the wisdom of the flesh," when he says: "The wisdom of the flesh is hostile to God; it does not submit to God's law, indeed it cannot."[16] It is voluntary consent, as I say, that distinguishes us from this last which we share with the animals.

DEFINITION OF VOLUNTARY CONSENT

For voluntary consent is a self-determining habit of the soul. Its action is neither forced nor extorted. It stems from the will and not from necessity, denying or giving itself on no issue except by way of the will. But if it is compelled in spite of itself, then there is violent, not voluntary, consent. Where

12. The terms *salus* and *salvari* have the technical meaning here of "wholeness" in the Christian sense, and "being made whole." Cf., for example, Acts 2:47 and 2 Cor 6:2. This will recur as the treatise develops. On the contemporary importance of this, and of the thought underlying it, see A. Forest's essay "S. Bernard et notre temps" in *S. Bernard Theologien*, ASOC 9 (1953) (Rome: Editiones Cistercienses, 1954), 294f.

13. The subtitles, 47 in number, are found in uniform style in at least 15 mss., including some of the most ancient, from all different regions. They have been retained in the critical edition as they are found in Dijon 658, and have been translated here, thus showing the text as it was commonly seen even in Bernard's time. See Leclercq's Introduction, OB 3:158-163.

14. On the place of this *naturalis appetitus* in Bernard's degrees of love, see P. Delfgaauw's essay in the work just cited, pp. 234-252, especially p. 238.

15. See Gal 5:17.

16. Rom 8:7.

the will is absent, so is consent; for only what is voluntary may be called consent. Hence, where you have consent, there also is the will. But where the will is, there is freedom. And this is what I understand by the term "free choice."

CHAPTER TWO

IN WHAT FREE CHOICE CONSISTS

F OR GREATER CLARITY, HOWEVER, and in order to be better equipped for what lies ahead, perhaps we should examine this somewhat more deeply. In the material world, life is not identical with sense-perception, not sense-perception with appetite; nor appetite with consent. This should become more evident from the definitions of each. For life in any body is an internal and natural movement, having existence only within the confines of that body.

DEFINITION OF SENSE

Whereas sense-perception is a vital movement in the body, alert and outward,

DEFINITION OF NATURAL APPETITE

And natural appetite, a force in a living being, intent on getting the senses moving,

DEFINITION OF CONSENT

Consent, on the other hand, is a spontaneous inclination of the will, or indeed, as I recall expressing it earlier, a self-determining habit of the soul.

DEFINITION OF WILL

Will is a rational movement, governing both sense-perception and appetite. In whatever direction it turns, it has reason
as its mate, one might even say as its follower. Not that it is
moved invariably by reason—indeed it does many things
through reason against reason, or, in other words, through
the medium of reason as it were, yet contrary to its counsel
and judgment—but it is never moved without reason. Hence it
is said: "The sons of this world are more prudent in their
own generation than the sons of light";[1] and again, "They
are wise in doing evil."[2] Indeed, prudence or wisdom cannot
be present in a creature, even in wrongdoing, by any means
other than by reason.

4. Reason is given to the will for instruction, not destruction. It would be to the destruction of the will, however,
were it to impose any necessity on it which would prevent it
from moving freely in accordance with its judgment. Such
necessity might push it (consenting to appetite or evil spirit)
toward wrong, making an animal of it, not knowing, or even
actively resisting the things which are of the Spirit of God; or
(following grace) toward right, making it spiritual, able to
judge all things, but itself judged by no one.[3] If, I say, the
will were incapable of reaching out to any of these because
of some prohibition of the reason, it would no longer be will.
For, the presence of necessity means the absence of will.

WITHOUT THE CONSENT OF ITS OWN WILL THE RATIONAL
CREATURE CAN NOT BE MADE JUST OR UNJUST

If the rational creature would, out of necessity and without
the consent of its own will, be made just or unjust, it ought
on no account to be dejected, nor could it possibly be elated,
since in either case that one faculty would be lacking which is

1. Lk 16:8.
2. Jer 4:22.
3. 1 Cor 2:14f.

capable in it of happiness or unhappiness, namely the will. Those other things listed above: life, sense-perception, and appetite, of themselves make one neither happy nor unhappy. Were this not so, trees because of their life, and animals because of the other two, would be subject to sorrow or worthy of beatitude; but this is out of the question. We have life in common with the trees, and sense-perception, appetite, and again, life with the animals; it is then what we call the will which distinguishes us from both of them. The consent of this will, voluntary, of course, and not necessary, proves us to be just or unjust, and also, meritedly, makes us happy or miserable. Such consent, on account of the imperishable freedom of the will and the inevitable judgment of the reason always and everywhere accompanying it, is, I think, well called free choice, having free disposal of itself because of the will and the power to judge of itself because of the reason. It is only right that judgment should accompany freedom, as whatever has the free disposal of itself, should it chance to sin, judges itself in the act of sinning. And it really is judgment, because if he sins, he suffers justly indeed, what he does not will, who does not sin unless he wills.

5. On what basis, in fact, can one impute anything to a man, whether good or bad, if he is not known to have the free disposal of himself? Necessity excuses from both. For necessity's presence means freedom's absence; and where there is no freedom, neither is there merit, nor consequently judgment, apart from the case of original sin, for that, clearly, is another matter. Moreover, whatever lacks this freedom of voluntary consent, lacks also undoubtedly merit and judgment. Hence, everything pertaining to man, will alone excepted, is free from both alike, since it has not the free disposal of itself. Thus life, sense-perception, appetite, memory, temperament, and the like, are subject to necessity to the extent that they are not fully subject to the will. But as to the will, since it is impossible for it not to obey itself—no one does not will what he wills, or wills what he does not will—so is it impossible for it to be deprived of its freedom.

AN ACT OF THE WILL CANNOT BE CHANGED EXCEPT
INTO ANOTHER ACT OF THE WILL

An act of the will can, indeed, be changed, but only into
another act of the will, so that freedom is never lost. The will
can thus no more be deprived of it than of itself. Should it
ever happen to be in man's power to will nothing at all, or to
will something but not by his willing faculty, then the will
would be capable of lacking freedom. That is why we impute
nothing they do, whether good or ill, to the mentally deficient, to infants, to the sleeping, because, even as they are no
longer masters of their reason, so neither do they retain the
use of their own will, nor consequently the judgment of freedom. Since, therefore, the will knows no freedom other than
itself, it is right that its judgment should arise only out of
itself. For never do dullness of wit, weakness of memory,
restlessness of appetite, obtuseness of sense-perception, nor
slackening of vitality of themselves constitute a person guilty,
even as their contraries do not make him innocent; and this
for no other reason than that all these are known to occur
necessarily at times, and without previous consultation of the
will.

CHAPTER THREE

A THREEFOLD FREEDOM: OF NATURE, OF GRACE, AND OF GLORY [1]

ONLY THE WILL, THEN, since, by reason of its innate freedom, it can be compelled by no force or necessity to dissent from itself, or to consent in any matter in spite of itself, makes a creature righteous or unrighteous, capable and deserving of happiness or of sorrow, insofar as it shall have consented to righteousness or unrighteousness. That is why we defined earlier on, —and not unsuitably I think, — such voluntary and free consent, on which every act of judgment, as we have seen, depends, as "free choice"; "free" referring to the will, "choice" to the reason. But free though it is, this does not signify the freedom of which the Apostle says: "Where the Spirit of the Lord is, there is freedom." [2]

FREEDOM FROM SIN

For here he means freedom from sin, as he points out elsewhere: "When you were slaves of sin, you were free in regard to righteousness. But now that you have been set free from sin and have become slaves of God, the return you get is sanctification and its end, eternal life." [3] Who in sinful flesh [4]

1. In his doctoral thesis, *Libero Arbitrio e Libertà della Grazia nel Pensiero di S. Bernardo*, (Rome: Ferrari, 1953), p. 17, Dom G. Venuta S O CIST. rightly observes that Bernard's teaching on freedom is an essential part of his mystical doctrine, and that both are a function of his monastic ideal.
2. 2 Cor 3:17.
3. Rom 6:20, 22.
4. Rom 8:3.

would claim to be free from sin? So I certainly do not believe that free choice takes its name from this type of freedom.

FREEDOM FROM SORROW

There is also a freedom from sorrow, of which the Apostle again says: "The creation itself will be set free from its bondage to decay and obtain the glorious liberty of the children of God."[5] But would anyone in this mortal condition dare arrogate to himself even this kind of freedom? Hence, we deny also that free choice takes its name from this freedom.

FREEDOM FROM NECESSITY

There is, however, a freedom which seems to me to fit it better, and which we might designate freedom fron necessity, since "necessary" appears to be contrary to "voluntary." What is done by necessity does not derive from the will, and vice versa.

A THREEFOLD FREEDOM

7. There are, then, these three forms of freedom, as they have occured to us: freedom from sin, from sorrow and from necessity. The last belongs to our natural condition; to the first we are restored by grace; and the second is reserved for us in our homeland.

THERE ARE SAID TO BE THREE LIBERTIES: THE FIRST, OF NATURE; THE SECOND, OF GRACE; THE THIRD, OF LIFE OR GLORY.

The first freedom, therefore, might be termed freedom of nature, the second of grace, the third of life or glory. For in the first place, we were created with free will and willing freedom, a creature noble in God's eyes. Secondly, we are re-formed in innocence, a new creature in Christ:[6] and

5. Rom 8:21.
6. 2 Cor 5:17; Gal 6:15.

thirdly, we are raised up to glory, a perfect creature in the Spirit. The first freedom is thus a title of considerable honor; the second, of even greater power; and the last, of total happiness. By the first, we have the advantage over other living things; by the second, over the flesh; while by the third, we cast down death itself.[7] Or, to express it another way, just as in the first, God put under our feet sheep and oxen and the beasts of the field,[8] so did he likewise, in the second, crush and lay low beneath our feet those spiritual beasts of the world of whom it is said: "Do not deliver the souls of those who trust in you to the wild beasts."[9] Finally, by the last-named, in our own more perfect submission to ourselves through victory over corruption and death—when, that is, death shall be last of all destroyed[10]—we will pass over into the glorious freedom of the sons of God,[11] the freedom by which Christ will set us free, when he delivers us as a kingdom to God the Father.[12] Of this, I think, and also of the one we have called freedom from sin, he said to the Jews: "If the Son makes you free, you will be free indeed."[13] He meant that even free choice stands in need of a liberator, but one, of course, who would set it free, not from necessity which was quite unknown to it since this pertains to the will, but rather from sin, into which it had fallen both freely and willingly, and also from the penalty of sin which it carelessly incurred and has unwillingly borne. From these two evils it was quite unable to extricate itself, except through him who alone of all men was made free among the dead;[14] free, that is, from sin in the midst of sinners.

8. He alone, indeed, among the sons of Adam was free from sin, he "who committed no sin; nor was there any guile found on his lips,"[15] he also possessed freedom from sorrow

7. See 1 Cor 15:26.
8. See Ps 8:8.
9. Ps 74:19.
10. 1 Cor 15:26.
11. Rom 8:21.
12. See 1 Cor 15:24.
13. Jn 8:36.
14. Ps 88:5 (Vg).
15. 1 Pet 2:22.

which is the penalty of sin, but this he possessed only in potency, not in act. Thus no one took away his life from him, but he laid it down of his own accord.[16] In a word, as the Prophet had foretold, "He was offered up because he willed it,"[17] and even as, at the time of his own choosing, he was "born of woman, born under the law, to redeem those who were under the law."[18] Hence, he, too, was subject to the law of suffering; but this was because he willed to be, in order that, himself free among sufferers and sinners, he might lift from his brothers' shoulders the yoke of both sin and suffering.

THE SAVIOR HAD THESE THREE LIBERTIES

He, therefore, enjoyed all three freedoms: the first by his human and divine nature combined, the others by his divine power. As to whether or not the first man was endowed with the last two in paradise, or how or to what extent he had them—of this, more presently.

16. Jn 10:18.
17. Isa 53:7 (Vg).
18. Gal 4:4f.

CHAPTER FOUR

WHAT KIND OF FREEDOM BELONGS TO THE HOLY SOULS IN THEIR DISEMBODIED STATE WHAT KIND BELONGS TO GOD AND WHAT KIND IS COMMON TO ALL RATIONAL CREATURES

THIS MUCH IS CERTAIN: that both these freedoms, from sin and suffering, are fully and perfectly present in those perfect souls who have been loosed from fleshly bonds, even as they are in God and his Christ, and the angels in heaven. For though the souls of the just, while they have not yet received their bodies, lack undoubtedly some measure of glory, they experience no trace of sorrow.

FREEDOM FROM NECESSITY IS IN BOTH GOOD AND EVIL RATIONAL CREATURES

Freedom from necessity belongs alike to God and to every rational creature, good or bad. Neither by sin nor by suffering is it lost or lessened; nor is it greater in the just man than in the sinner, nor fuller in the angel than in man. For the consent of the human will, which is directed by grace toward the good, makes man freely good, and, in the good, free, by the fact that it is voluntarily given and not unwillingly dragged out. In the same way, when it inclines willingly toward the bad, it makes man nonetheless free and spontaneous in the bad. He is not forced to be evil by some other cause, but simply chooses to be so at the behest of his own will. And just as the angels in heaven, or even God himself, remain freely good, that is, by their own will, not from any extrinsic necessity; so the devil freely both opted for evil and persists in it, not by coercion from without, but of his own free choice. Freedom of will thus continues to exist, even where the mind is captive, as full in the bad as in the good, yet more orderly in the good; and as complete in its own way in the creature as in the Creator, yet more powerfully in the Creator.[1]

10. When a person complains and says: "I *wish* I could have a good will, but I just can't manage it," this in no way argues against the freedom of which we have been speaking, as if the will thus suffered violence or were subject to necessity. Rather is he witnessing to the fact that he lacks that freedom which is called freedom from sin. Because, whoever wants to have a good will proves thereby that he has a will, since his desire is aimed at good only through his will. And if he finds himself unable to have a good will whereas he really wants to, then this is because he feels freedom is lacking to him, freedom namely from sin, by which it pains him that his will is oppressed, though not suppressed.[2] Indeed it is more than likely that, since he wants to have a good will, he does, in fact, to some extent, have it. What he wants is good, and he could hardly want good otherwise than by means of good will; just as he could want evil only by a bad will. When we desire good, then our will is good; when evil, evil. In either case, there is will; and everywhere freedom; necessity yields to will. But if we are unable to do what we will, we feel that freedom itself is somehow captive to sin, or that it is unhappy, not that it is lost.

11. In my opinion, therefore, free choice takes its name from that freedom alone by which the will is free either to judge itself good if it has consented to good, or bad, if to evil; only by willing, in fact, can it feel itself to consent to either. For freedom from sin might, perhaps, more fittingly be called free counsel; and freedom from sorrow, free pleasure, rather than free choice.

1. E. Gilson compares this passage with Descartes teaching on liberty, *La Liberté chez Descartes et la théologie,* (Paris: Alcan, 1913), pp. 230-243.

2. "Premi non perimi." W. W. Williams observes, "The *jeu de mots* is singularly happy, but difficult to render in English. 'Suppress' is strong enough, if we remember the original sense of *supprimo,* to sink a ship to the bottom of the sea." *The Treatise of St Bernard Concerning Grace and Free Will,* (London: Society for Promoting Christian Knowlege, 1920), p. 19, note 2.

JUDGMENT, COUNSEL, AND PLEASURE

Choice is an act of judgment. But even as it belongs to judgment to distinguish between what is lawful and what not, so it belongs to counsel to examine what is expedient and what not, and to pleasure, to experience what is pleasant and what not. If only we took counsel for our profit as freely as we judge our deeds! so that, as we freely distinguish by our judgment between right and wrong, we might also, by counsel, choose the licit as more suitable and reject the illicit as harmful. Then we would not only be free in our choice, but undoubtedly also free in counsel, and consequently, free from sin. But, supposing all and only that which was expedient or lawful gained our assent? Might we not in this case be also regarded as free with respect to pleasure, feeling as we do that we are free from everything that could displease, in other words from every sorrow? Now, however, since we discern many things by means of the judgment as either to be done or omitted, which we nevertheless choose or reject through counsel in a manner quite at variance with the rectitude of our judgment; and since, again, we do not freely embrace as pleasing all that we observe with counsel as being right and suitable, but impatiently endure it, rather, as something hard and burdensome; it is evident that we possess neither free counsel nor free pleasure.

12. Another question concerns whether Adam possessed these prior to sin. This we shall discuss in due course. But one thing is certain: we *shall* possess them when, by God's mercy, we shall obtain what we pray for: "Thy will be done, on earth as it is in heaven."[3] This shall come to pass when that which appears, as has been said, common to every rational creature, namely, a choice which is free from necessity, shall be in the elect of the human race also—as it is already in the holy angels—secure from sin and safe from sorrow, the happy experience of that threefold liberty proving what is the will of God, good, acceptable and perfect.[4] In the meantime, this

3. Mt 6:10.
4. See Rom 12:2.

is not yet so; in its full measure, men have only freedom of choice. Freedom of counsel they possess merely in part, —that is, the few spiritual ones among them, who have crucified their flesh with its passions and desires,[5] so that sin no longer reigns in their mortal body.[6] Now, it is freedom of counsel which brings it about that sin does not so reign. That it still has some small hold is due to the fact of free choice's still being captive. "But when the perfect comes, then the imperfect will pass away."[7] This means: when freedom of counsel shall have been fully achieved, the judgment's shackles shall also fall away. And that is what we daily ask in prayer, when we say to God: "Thy kingdom come."[8] This kingdom is not yet wholly established among us. But it comes closer by degrees each day, and, daily more and more it gradually extends its bounds. It does so in those only whose interior self, with the help of God, is renewed from day to day.[9] In the measure, therefore, that grace's kingdom is extended, sin's power is weakend. It is a process which is still unfinished because of this perishable body which weighs down the soul[10] and because of the needy condition of this earthly dwelling[11] which burdens the mind full of thoughts.[12] Even those who appear more perfect in this mortal state have to acknowledge that "In many things we all offend"[13] and "if we say we have no sin, we deceive ourselves, and the truth is not in us."[14] That is why they pray without ceasing:[15] "Thy kingdom come."[16] But this will not be accomplished even in them until not only has sin no further sway over their perishable body,[17] but also there neither is nor can be any sin at all in the body, then immortal.

5. See Gal 5:24.
6. See Rom 6:12.
7. See 1 Cor 13:10.
8. Mt 6:10.
9. See 2 Cor 4:16.
10. See Wis 9:15; Rom 7:24.
11. See Wis 9:15; 2 Cor 5:1; 2 Pet 1:13.
12. See Wis 9:15.
13. Jas 3:2.
14. 1 Jn 1:8.
15. See 1 Thess 5:17.
16. Mt 6:10.
17. See Rom 6:12.

CHAPTER FIVE

WHETHER FREEDOM FROM SORROW OR FREEDOM
OF COUNSEL IS GRANTED IN THIS WORLD

WHAT NOW SHALL WE SAY about freedom of pleasure in this present evil age[1] where the day's own trouble is scarcely sufficient for the day,[2] where every creature groans and is in labor until now, subjected as it is to futility not of its own will,[3] where the life of man is a hard service upon the earth,[4] where even the spiritual, who have already received the first fruits of the Spirit, groan inwardly, awaiting the redemption of their body?[5] Can there really be room in such a situation for this type of freedom? What is left free for our good pleasure, I ask, where every square inch seems taken up by sorrow? Indeed, here not even innocence or righteousness are immune to sorrow (any more than they are to sin), where the just man cries out: "Wretched man that I am! Who will deliver me from this body of death?"[6] And again: "My tears have been my food day and night."[7] Where night follows day and day night in one rhythm of sorrow, there is no moment's room for real pleasure. Lastly, all who desire to live a godly life in Christ will suffer persecution[8] most of all, since judgment begins with the household of God,[9] as he commanded, saying: "Begin at my sanctuary."[10]

1. See Gal 1:4.
2. See Mt 6:34.
3. See Rom 8:20-22.
4. See Job 7:1.
5. See Rom 8:23.

6. Rom 7:24.
7. Ps 42:3.
8. See 2 Tim 3:12.
9. See 1 Pet 4:17.
10. Ezek 9:6.

14. Yet, though virtue is not immune, perhaps vice is; and at times, at rest from sorrow, feels the touch of pleasure? No, indeed. For those who rejoice in doing evil, and delight in the worst sort of things,[11] imitate the wild laughter of the mad. For no sorrow is more truly sorrow than false joy. And the more in this a thing wears the guise of happiness, the more actually is it misery. As the Wise Man says: "It is better to go to the house of mourning than to go to the house of feasting."[12]

CORPORAL JOY IS NOT WITHOUT SORROW

A certain pleasure is to be found in goods of the body, namely in eating, drinking, warm clothing, and in other such nutriments or coverings of the flesh. But do even these, in fact, escape from sorrow? Bread is fine, but to one who is hungry; drink delightful, but to the thirsty. To the sated, food and drink are a burden, not a joy. Once hunger has been eased, bread will mean little to you; thirst slaked, even the most limpid stream will no more attract you than a swamp. Only those who are hot seek the shade; only the cold or those in darkness hail the sun. None of these things pleases without the prick of necessity. Take this away, and at once the pleasure itself which seemed to form part of them yields to tedium and distate.

A CONCLUSION

It must therefore be admitted here, again, that everything belonging to the present life involves suffering. The only mitigating factor is that, in the relentless hardships which go with our more difficult undertakings, lighter tasks come as a sort of relaxation. In a given time and situation, while heavy and light alternate, the experience of the light seems to provide an interlude to sorrow, as when sometimes we think it a joy when we pass out of the doldrums of nerve-racking trials into worries of a milder kind.

---

11. See Prov 2:14.   12. Eccles 7:2.

THOSE TAKEN UP IN CONTEMPLATION ENJOY
THE FREEDOM OF PLEASURE

15. But what of those who, at times, being caught up in the Spirit through excess of contemplation, become capable of savoring something of the sweetness of heavenly bliss? Do these attain to freedom from sorrow as often as this happens to them? Yes, indeed. Even in this present life, those who with Mary have chosen the better part, which shall not be taken away from them,[13] enjoy freedom of pleasure; rarely, however, and fleetingly. This is undeniable. For those who now possess that which shall never be taken away, plainly experience what is to come: in a word, happiness. And since happiness and sorrow are incompatible, through the Spirit they participate in the former, as often as they cease to feel the latter. Hence, on this earth, contemplatives alone can in some way enjoy freedom of pleasure, though only in part,[14] in very small part, and on the rarest occasions.

THE JUST IN NO SMALL PART ENJOY FREEDOM OF COUNSEL

As to freedom of counsel: every righteous man enjoys it, in part again, but in no small part.

FREEDOM OF CHOICE

Furthermore, as was evident in what we said earlier, freedom of choice belongs to everyone who has the use of reason; no less, essentially, to the bad than to the good; as fully in this life as in the next.

---

13. See Lk 10:42.   14. See 1 Cor 13:9-12.

CHAPTER SIX

GRACE IS NECESSARY IN ORDER THAT WE MAY WILL WHAT IS GOOD

I THINK IT HAS BEEN CLEARLY SHOWN that even freedom of choice is to some extent held captive as long as it is unaccompanied or imperfectly accompanied by the two remaining freedoms; and that from no other cause arises this frailty of ours of which the Apostle speaks: "So that you do not the things you would."[1] To will lies in our power indeed as a result of free choice, but not to carry out what we will. I am not saying to will the good or to will the bad, but simply to will. For to will the good indicates an achievement; and to will the bad, a defect; whereas simply to will denotes the subject itself which does either the achieving or the failing. To this subject, however, creating grace gives existence. Saving grace gives it the achievement. But when it fails, it is to blame for its own failure. Free choice, accordingly, constitutes us willers; grace, willers of the good. Because of our willing faculty, we are able to will; but because of grace, to will the good. Just as, simply to fear is one thing, and to fear God, another; to love, one, and to love God, another, —since to fear and to love, on their own. signify affections, but, coupled with the additional word "God," virtues, —so also will is one thing, and to will the good, another.

17. For mere affections live naturally in us, as of us, but those additional acts, as of grace. This means only that grace sets in order what creation has given, so that virtues are no-

1. See Gal 5:17.

thing else than ordered affections. It is written of certain people that they were in great fear where there was no cause for fear;[2] they feared, that is, but inordinately. It was this that our Lord wanted to set in order in his disciples when he said: "I will show you whom you should fear,"[3] and David: "Come, children," he said, "listen to me; I will teach you the fear of the Lord."[4] He was also reproving men on the score of inordinate love who said: "I have come as a light into this world, and men loved darkness rather than light."[5] That is why the Bride says in the Song: "Set charity in order in me."[6] So, too, those were being cautioned about inordinate desire to whom it was said: "You do not know what you are asking;"[7] but were shown how to bring their crooked wills back to straight path when they heard: "Are you able to drink the cup that I am to drink? "[8] Again he taught them— at the time by word, but later by example also—how to set their will in order, when, at the beginning of his passion, praying that the cup might pass from him, he immediately added: "Nevertheless, not as I will; but as you will."[9] Thus we have received from God as part of our natural condition how to will, how to fear and how to love. In this we are creatures. But how to will the good, and how to fear God, and how to love God, we receive with grace's touch: in this we are creatures of God.

THE DIFFERENCE BETWEEN A GOOD AND A BAD FREE WILL

18. Created, then, to a certain extent, as our own in free-dom of will, we become God's as it were by good will. More-

2. See Ps 53:5 (Vg).
3. Lk 12:5.
4. Ps 34:11.
5. See Jn 3:19.
6. See Song 2:4 (Vg); and Bernard's "Apology to Abbot William," tr. Michael Casey, *The Works of Bernard of Clairvaux,* vol. 1, CF 1 (Spencer, Massachusetts, Cistercian Publications, 1970), p. 42, note 47. There is a whole subsection de-voted to this ordering of charity, in P. Delfgaauw's study, "La Nature et les Degrés de l'Amour selon S. Bernard," *S. Bernard Théologien,* ASOC 9 (1953), 295-251. See also ibid., p. 274.
7. Mt 20:22.
8. Mt 20:22.
9. Mt 26:39.

over he makes the will good, who made it free; and makes it
good to this end, that we may be a kind of first fruits of his
creatures;[10] because it would have been better for us never to
have existed than that we should remain always our own. For
those who wished to belong to themselves, became indeed
like gods, knowing good and evil; but then they were not
merely their own, but the devil's.[11] Hence, free will makes us
our own; bad will, the devil's; and good will, God's. This is
the meaning of the words: "The Lord knows those who are
his."[12] For to those who are not his he says: "Amen I say to
you, I do not know you."[13] As long, therefore, as by bad will
we belong to the devil, we are, in a certain sense, no longer
God's; just as, when by good will we pass over to God, we
cease to belong to the devil. "No one," in fact, "can serve
two masters."[14] Furthermore, whether we belong to God or
to the devil, this does not prevent us from being also our
own. For on either side freedom of choice continues to
operate, and so the ground of merit remains, inasmuch as,
when we are bad we are rightly punished, since we have
become so of our own free choice, or when we are good we
are glorified, since we could not have become so without a
similar decision of our will. It is our own will that enslaves us
to the devil, not his power; whereas, God's grace subjects us
to God, not our own will. Our will, created good (as must be
granted) by the good God, shall nevertheless be perfect only
when perfectly subjected to its Creator. This does not mean
that we ascribe to it its own perfection, and to God, only its
creation; since to be perfect is far more than to be made. The
attributing to God of what is less excellent, and to ourselves
of what is more, surely stands condemned in the very statement. Finally, the Apostle, feeling what he really was by
nature and what he hoped to be by grace, said: "I can will
what is right, but I cannot do it."[15] He realised that to will

10. See Jas 1:18.
11. See Gen 3:5.
12. 2 Tim 2:19.
13. Mt 25:12.
14. Mt 6:24.
15. Rom 7:18.

was possible to him as a result of free choice, but that for this will to be perfect he stood in need of grace. For, if to will what is evil is a defect of the willing faculty, then undoubtedly to will what is good marks a growth in this same faculty. To measure up to every good thing that we will, however, is its perfection.

19. In order, then, that our willing, derived from our free choice may be perfect, we need the twofold gift of grace: namely, true wisdom, which means the turning of the will to good, and full power, which means its confirmation in good.[16]

PERFECT GOOD WILL: A THREEFOLD GOOD

Now, perfect conversion is conversion to good, to the end that only fitting or permissible things may be found pleasing; and perfect confirmation in good is to the end that nothing of what is pleasing may any longer be found wanting. Then, in the end, shall the will be perfect, when it shall be fully whole and wholly full.[17] From the first moment of its existence, it possesses in itself a twofold goodness: the one, general, by the mere fact of creation, which means that anything created by a good God cannot be other than good (for "God saw everything he had made, and, behold, they were very good"[18]); the other, special, arising from its freedom of choice, by which it was made in the image of him who created it.[19] And if to these two goods we add a third, conversion

16. It is difficult to find a good rendering here. Since two key-terms are involved, it seems best to give Bernard's own sentence: "Ut ergo velle nostrum, quod ex libero arbitrio habemus, perfectum habeamus, duplici gratiae munere indigemus, et vero videlicet sapere, quod est voluntatis ad bonum conversio, et pleno etiam posse, quod est eiusdem in bono confirmatio." According to W. Williams, *The Treatise*, p. 33, note 1, whose translation I have adopted, "these (*vero sapere pleno posse*) would appear to be two of the gifts of the Holy Ghost, *sapientia* and *fortitudo*."

17. Again, it is not easy to do justice to Bernard's clever juggling: " . . . cum plene fuerit bona, et bene plena." W. Williams, *The Treatise*, p. 33, note 2, comments: "The 'plene bona' refers to *conversio*, and the 'bene plena' to *confirmatio*, which together effect the perfection of the will in the moral as distinct from the natural sphere."

18. Gen 1:31.

19. See Gen 1:26.

to the Creator, then it may rightly be regarded as perfectly good: good, that is, as part of a good creation; better within its own sphere of action; best in its being established in order. This latter implies the total conversion of the will to God, and its wholehearted, voluntary and devoted subjection. To such perfection of righteousness is due, and, in fact, is joined, the fullness of glory, because these two are so closely inter-related that neither can there be perfection of righteousness apart from fullness of glory, nor fullness of glory without perfect righteousness. In fine, righteousness of this kind can-not exist outside of glory, since glory can only be predicated of such righteousness. Wherefore it is well stated: "Blessed are those who hunger and thirst for righteousness, for they shall be satisfied."[20]

20. These are the two qualities mentioned above, true wis-dom, namely, and full power; wisdom referring to righteous-ness, and power to glory. But the terms "true" and "full" are added, the one in order to distinguish it from the wisdom of the flesh, which is death,[21] and from the wisdom of the world, which is folly with God,[22] and by which men are wise after their own fashion; (wise, that is, in performing evil[23]); and the other, to distinguish it from the power of those of whom it is said: "The powerful shall be powerfully tor-mented."[24] For neither true wisdom nor full power is to be found except when those two freedoms mentioned earlier, (namely, freedom of counsel and freedom of pleasure), form a combination with free choice. Now, I would regard as truly wise and fully powerful only the man who not merely is able to will a thing from his free choice,[25] but is able also, by

20. Mt 5:6.
21. See Rom 8:6 (Vg, followed by Bernard, uses *sapientia carnis* in Rom 8:7, and *prudentia carnis* in 8:6. The Greek has *phronema tes sarkos* in both cases, meaning "the general bent of thought, the practical tendency and effort of the Flesh" (Boylan, *St Paul's Epistle to the Romans,* [Dublin: Gill and Son, 1947], p. 134).
22. See 1 Cor 3:19.
23. See Jer 4:22.
24. See Wis 6:6 (Vg). The play is on the verb *posse* used above in contrast to *sapere* (see note 84); whence, *potentes potentor tormenta patientur* (Wis 6:6).
25. See Rom 7:18.

virtue of the remaining two, to do it. He would in this case be neither capable of willing what is evil, nor of lacking what he willed; the former, resulting from freedom of counsel, being true wisdom; the latter, from freedom of pleasure, full power. But what man is of such quality and so great that he can glory in this? [26] Or where, or when may it be obtained? Is it in this age? Indeed, did such a one live, he would be better than Paul, who openly confessed: "I cannot do it."[27] Can it be said of Adam in paradise? If it could, he would never have suffered exile from paradise.

26. See 1 Cor: 3:21.
27. See Rom 7:18.

CHAPTER SEVEN

WHETHER ADAM IN PARADISE WAS ENDOWED WITH THIS THREEFOLD FREEDOM HOW FAR HIS ENDOWMENT WAS LOST BY SIN

THE TIME HAS COME to examine what we put off doing earlier: whether the first human beings in paradise possessed all three of the freedoms referred to, freedom of choice, of counsel and of pleasure, or, in other words, freedom from necessity, from sin and from sorrow, or whether they had only two, or even only one of them. With regard to the first, there is no difficulty, when we recall how the argument already advanced has shown it clearly to exist in the just and sinners alike. Concerning the remaining two, it may fairly be asked whether Adam possessed them, either both or even one. Because, if he had neither, what did he lose? He certainly retained his freedom of choice, unharmed by the fact of his sin. If, then, he lost nothing, what difference did it make to him being expelled from paradise? But if he possessed any one of them, how did he lost it? For it is beyond doubt that, from the mere fact of sinning, he was, in the body, neither free from sin nor from sorrow. Besides, either of them once received, it could never be lost. Otherwise, neither his wisdom nor his power could be shown to have been perfect in the way defined above, as long as he could will what he ought not to will, and receive what he did not want to receive. Or is it that he had them in a certain measure, but could lose them because he did not possess them fully?

78

FREEDOM OF COUNSEL AND FREEDOM OF PLEASURE, EACH HAS TWO DEGREES

The fact is that each of them admits of two degrees, a higher and a lower. The higher freedom of counsel consists in not being able to sin, the lower in being able not to sin.[1] Again, the higher freedom of pleasure lies in not being able to be disturbed, the lower in being able not to be disturbed.[2] Thus, man received in his very nature, along with full freedom of choice, the lower degree of each of these freedoms; and when he sinned, fell from both. In losing completely his freedom of counsel, he fell from being able not to sin to not being able not to sin. Likewise, from being able not to be disturbed, he fell to not being able not to be disturbed, with the total loss of his freedom of pleasure. There only remained, for his punishment, the freedom of choice through which he had lost the others; that he could not lost. Enslaved by his own will to sin,[3] he deservedly forfeited freedom of counsel. Through his sin he became a debtor of death,[4] so how could he hold on to his freedom of pleasure?

22. Three freedoms he had received. By abusing the one called freedom of choice, he deprived himself of the others. He abused it, in that what he had received for his glory, he turned to his shame, in accordance with the words of Scripture: "Man, when he was in honor, did not understand; he became like the senseless beasts."[5] Among all living beings, to man alone was given the ability to sin, as part of his prerogative of free choice. But he was given it, not that he might, but rather that he might appear the more glorious did he not sin when he was capable of doing so. What, in fact, could afford him greater glory than that Scripture's words be spoken of him, where it says: "Who is he, and we shall praise him?"[6] But why such praise? "For he has done wonderful

---

1. See Augustine, *Of Correction and Grace* 12:33, for the same distinction.
2. Or, "to be upset," "made sorrowful."
3. See Rom 6:17f.
4. See Rom 5:12.
5. Ps 49:12 (Vg).
6. Sir 31:9f (Vg).

things in his life."[7] What kind of things? "He had the power to transgress," it says, "and he did not transgress, and to do evil and did not do it."[8] This honor he kept as long as he was sinless; but once he sinned, he lost it. He sinned, because he was free to sin, and free from no other source than his own freedom of choice, which bore within it the possibility of sinning. No failure this of the bestower, but rather of the abuser, who made over to the service of sin that faculty he had received for the glory of not sinning. For, though the root of his sin lay in the ability received, yet he sinned, not because he was able to, but because he willed to. So it was that, when the devil and his angels rebelled, others of their company refused to do so: not because they could not, but because they would not.

23. The sinner's fall, therefore, was not due to the gift of being able to, but to the vice of willing to. However, if he fell by the power of his will, this does not mean that he was equally free to rise again by that same power. The ability to remain standing lest he fall[9] was indeed given to his will, but not to get up again once he fell. It is not as easy to climb out of a pit as to fall into one. By his will alone, man fell into the pit of sin; but he cannot climb out of his will alone, since now, even if he wishes he cannot not sin.

7. Ibid.
8. Ibid.
9. See 1 Cor 10:12.

CHAPTER EIGHT

FREE CHOICE REMAINS AFTER SIN HAS TAKEN OVER

DOES THE FACT that he cannot not sin, then, put an end to free choice? No; but he lost free counsel by which previously he had enjoyed the ability not to sin. In the same way, the poor wretch may attribute his not being able any longer not to be disturbed to the fact that he has also lost freedom of pleasure by means of which previously he was able not to be disturbed.

ALTHOUGH MAN CANNOT SIN, NEVERTHELESS HE HAS NOT LOST FREE CHOICE

Free choice, consequently, still remains, even after man's sin, tinged with sorrow but intact. And the fact that he can in no way extricate himself either from sin or sorrow signifies, not the destruction of free choice, but the privation of the other two freedoms. For it does not belong to free choice, in itself, nor did it ever belong to it, to possess either power or wisdom, but only to will; nor can it make a creature wise or able, but only willing. He cannot therefore be considered as having lost free choice, if he has ceased to be wise or able, but only if he has ceased to be willing. For where there is no will, neither is there freedom. I am not saying that once a person ceases to will the good, but once he ceases simply to will—where it is not merely a question of the good ceasing in the will, but of the will itself ceasing in its entirety—must free choice also be said unquestionably to vanish. If he finds himself unable simply to will the good, this is a sign that he lacks

free counsel, not free choice. And if he finds himself powerless, not indeed to will the good, but to accomplish that good
which he already wills, let him recognise that it is not free
choice that is wanting to him, but free pleasure. Hence, if
free choice so follows the will everywhere that unless the will
ceases to function free choice will continue to operate, then
the will remains present equally in evil and in good; and free
choice likewise in evil and in good. And, as the will, even in a
state of sorrow, does not cease for all that to be the will, but
is called, and is in fact, a sorrowful will, (as it is also called,
and is, a happy will), so neither can any adversity or necessity
either destroy, or, in what concerns its own nature, in any
way diminish, freedom of choice.

25. But though it always carries on unimpaired, it cannot
of itself rise from evil to good as easily as it could of itself fall
from good to evil. And what wonder is it if it is unable to rise
of itself from its fallen condition, when in its standing it was
quite powerless to advance on its own to something better?
In a word, while to some extent it still enjoyed those other
two freedoms, it could not ascend from these lower degrees
to the higher, that is, from a state of being able not to sin and
being able not to be disturbed to that of not being able to sin
and not being able to be disturbed. Now, if with the help,
even in some small measure, of those freedoms, it was yet
unable to raise itself from the good to the better, how much
less chance does it stand, now that it is deprived of them, of
raising itself up by its own power from evil to that former
level which was good.

26. And this is where Christ comes in. In him, man possesses the necessary "power of God and the wisdom of
God,"[1] who, inasmuch as he is wisdom, pours back into man
true wisdom, and so restores to him his free counsel; and,
inasmuch as he is power, renews his full power, and so restores to him his free pleasure. As a result, being by the
former perfectly good, he may now no longer know sin; and
being, by the latter, completely happy, may no longer feel its

1. 1 Cor 1:24.

sting. Such perfection, nevertheless, must be awaited in the next life, when both these freedoms, at present lost, will be fully restored to free choice, not as it is given to any just man here on earth however perfect, and not as it was given even to the first human beings to enjoy them in paradise, but as the angels possess them now in heaven. Meanwhile, in "this body of death"[2] and in "the present evil age,"[3] we must be content simply with not giving way to sin from any concupiscence, and this we may do through our freedom of counsel; and with fearing no adversity for the sake of righteousness, and this we may do through our freedom of pleasure. In this sinful flesh,[4] however, and in this evil of the day,[5] it is no small wisdom not to consent to sin, though one cannot be rid of it altogether; and it is no inconsiderable power, manfully to despise adversity for the sake of truth, though one cannot yet, in happiness, avoid feeling it at times.

27. Here below, we must learn from our freedom of counsel not to abuse free choice, in order that one day we may be able fully to enjoy freedom of pleasure. Thus we are repairing the image of God in us, and the way is being paved, by grace, for the retrieving of that former honor which we forfeited by sin. Happy then will be the man who shall deserve to hear said of him: "Who is he, and we shall praise him? For he has done wonderful things in his life: who had the power to transgress, and did not transgress; to do evil and did not do it."[6]

2. See Rom 7:24.
3. Gal 1:4.
4. See Rom 8:3.

5. See Mt 6:34.
6. Sir 31:9f.

CHAPTER NINE

THE IMAGE AND LIKENESS OF THE CREATOR CONSIST IN THIS THREEFOLD FREEDOM

I BELIEVE THAT in these three freedoms there is con-
contained the image and likeness of the Creator in which
we were made;[1] that in freedom of choice lies the image,
and in the other two is contained a certain twofold likeness.
Maybe, therefore, the reason why free choice alone suffers no
lessening or falling away, is that in it, more than in the
others, there seems to be imprinted some substantial image of
the eternal and immutable deity.

FREE CHOICE IS LIKE ETERNITY

For, although it had a beginning, it knows no end, nor has
it experience either of increase through righteousness or
glory, nor decrease through sin or sorrow. What could be
more like eternity without actually being eternity? Now, in
the other two freedoms, liable not only to partial diminution
but even to total loss, one sees, added to the image, a certain
more accidental likeness of the divine power and wisdom. By
a fault we lost them; by grace, we recovered them; and daily,
each in varying degrees, either advance in them or fall away.
They may be even irreparably lost; but also securely possessed, beyond the bounds of diminution.

29. Man was set in paradise, not indeed in the highest grade
of this twofold likeness to the wisdom and power of God,
but in a state quite close to it. For what could be closer to

1. See Gen 1:26.

not being able to sin or to be disturbed—in which condition, undoubtedly, the holy angels now live and God has lived always—than being able not to sin and not to be disturbed, in which state man was created? From this he fell away through sin and we along with him and in him only, through grace, to regain of it, not indeed the fullness, but some lower grade instead. True, we cannot be completely without sin or sorrow here on earth but we can, with the help of grace, avoid being overcome either by sin or by sorrow. Nevertheless, though Scripture says: "No one born of God commits sin,"[2] this refers to those only who are predestined to life: not that they never sin, but that sin is not imputed to them either because it is atoned for by due penance, or is covered up by charity. "Charity," as we know, "covers a multitude of sins,"[3] and: "Blessed is he whose transgression is forgiven, whose sin is covered," and: "Blessed is the man to whom the Lord imputes no guilt."[4]

BERNARD BEAUTIFULLY DISCERNS THE GRADES OF RATIONAL CREATURES

The highest angels, therefore, possess the highest grade of divine likeness, we the lowest; Adam enjoyed a degree somewhere in between, but the devils none whatever. For to the heavenly spirits it was given to persevere untouched by sin and sorrow; to Adam, to be without them admittedly, but not to persevere; and to us, not even to be without them, but only to be able not to yield to them. As the devil and his members, moreover, never will to resist sin, so neither are they ever able to escape its punishment.

FREE COUNSEL AND FREE PLEASURE DENOTE GOD'S LIKENESS AND FREE CHOICE HIS IMAGE

30. Both these freedoms (of counsel and of pleasure) by means of which true wisdom and power is communicated to

2. 1 Jn 3:9.
3. 1 Pet 4:8.
4. Ps 32:1f.

the rational creature God has dispensed according to his will and according to the way they were to vary in relation to causes, places, and times, inasmuch as they were possessed in slight measure on earth, more generously in paradise, fully in heaven, and not at all in hell. Freedom of choice, on the other hand, was never to change from the state in which it was created, but was always, considered in its own nature, equally present, whether in heaven or on earth or in hell. So it is that the other two freedoms correspond to God's likeness, but freedom of choice to his image. And, in fact, there is Scriptural testimony to show that, in hell, both those freedoms disappear, the ones, namely, which are said to pertain to his likeness. True wisdom (which, as we saw, is connected with freedom of counsel) disappears, as is clearly testified where we read: "Whatever your hand finds to do, do it with your might; for there is no work or thought or knowledge or wisdom in hell, to which you are going."[5] And of power, which is bestowed with freedom of pleasure, the Gospel says: "Bind him hand and foot, and cast him into the outer darkness."[6] What else does this binding of hand and foot mean than the utter privation of power?

EVIL WILL JUSTLY CONTINUES IN HELL,
REBELLING AGAINST ITS PUNISHMENT

31. But someone may say: "How can it be that there is no element of wisdom there, when the ills which have to be borne must surely force one to repent of the evil conduct of the past? Can anyone not repent amid such sufferings? Or, on the other hand, can repentance for evil behavior possibly not include an alloy of wisdom? " This would certainly be a valid objection, if the sinful act alone were punished, and not the bad will. No one doubts the impossibility in those torments of finding pleasure in the repetition of the sinful act. Nevertheless, if the will remains evil even in hell's anguish,

5. Eccles 9:10.
6. Mt 22:13.

what weight can the denial of the act carry? Or how can anyone regard it as wise, merely because it has no inclination to indulge itself amid the flames? In fine, "Wisdom will not enter an ill-willed soul."[7] But how are we to prove that ill-will continues even in such sufferings? Well, to mention nothing else, they (the damned) are quite unwilling to be punished. Now, it is only right that people who have done things deserving of punishment should be punished. This means that they do not will what is right. And the more discordant it is with righteousness, the more is the will unrighteous, and consequently evil. There are two things which indicate an unrighteous will: delight in sinning and in having sinned without paying the penalty. What trace of true wisdom or of good will is to be found in such as take pleasure in sinning as long as it lies in their power, and when they are no longer able to, want nothing more than that their guilty past be left unavenged? But granted, for argument's sake, that they are sorry for having sinned, would they not still prefer to sin again had they the option, rather than to undergo sin's punishment? Yet, the former is wicked; the latter, righteous. When did a good will ever choose more what was wrong than what was right? Besides, those are not really sorry who do not grieve as much over the fact of having lived selfishly as over not being able to continue so doing. One last point: from the outside one can recognize the inside. As long as the body goes on burning in hellfire, so long is it evident that the will is fixed in malice. Accordingly, of the likeness contained in the freedoms of counsel and of pleasure, nothing remains or can remain in hell. But the image remains, even there, in free choice, permanent and unchanged.

7. Wis 1:4.

CHAPTER TEN

THROUGH CHRIST THE LIKENESS WHICH PROPERLY BELONGS
TO THE DIVINE IMAGE IS RESTORED IN US

NOT EVEN IN THIS PRESENT WORLD could the proper likeness be found, however, even the image would still have lain stained and deformed, had not that woman of the Gospel lit her lamp[1] (had Wisdom not appeared in the flesh, in other words), swept the house (of the vices), searched carefully for her lost coin (her image) which, its original luster gone, coated over with the skin of transgression, lay buried as it were in the dust; having found it, had she not not wiped it clean and taken it away from the "region of un-likeness;"[2] then, refashioned in its erstwhile beauty, made it like the saints in glory;[3] were she not, indeed, some day to make it quite conformable to herself—on that day, namely, when the words of Scripture would be fulfilled: "We know that when he appears we shall be like him, for we shall see him as he is."[4] To whom, in fact, could this work be better suited than to the Son of God, who, being the splendor and the figure of the Father's substance,[5] upholding all things by his word, was well qualified for it, from both these standpoints. So he was able to reform what was deformed, strengthen what was weak, and, dispelling with the godhead's splendor the shadows of sin, to make man wise, and, by the might of his word, to lend him strength against the tyranny of the demons.

1. See Lk 15:8.
2. See E. Gilson, op. cit., p. 45f.
3. See Sir 45:2 (Vg).

4. 1 Jn 3:2.
5. See Heb 1:3 (Vg).

33. That very form came,[6] therefore, to which free choice was to be conformed, because in order that it might regain its original form, it had to be reformed from that out of which it had been formed. Now, wisdom is the form and conformation means that the image fulfills in the body what form does in the world. Form "reaches mightily from one end to the other, and orders all things gently."[7] From end to end it reaches: that is, from the end of the heavens to the lower parts of the earth,[8] from the highest angel to the smallest worm. It reaches mightily, not indeed by moving about or filling up places, nor by mere official administration of its subject creature, but by a certain substantial and omnipresent strength, with which, undoubtedly, it powerfully moves, orders and administers all things. It is not forced to do this by any inner compulsion. Nor does it labor in its activity under the strain, but with tranquil intent orders all things gently. Again, it reaches from end to end: that is, from creation's birth to the end appointed by its Creator. This may be either the end to which nature impels it, or that which the cause speeds along, or that which grace concedes.[9] And it reaches mightily, since none of these is reached without its having been preordained by a most powerful providence in accordance with its will.[10]

34. This is the way, then, in which free choice should try to govern its body, as wisdom does the world, reaching mightily from end to end, or in other words so strongly commanding each sense and each member that it will not suffer sin to reign in its mortal body,[11] nor give its members over as instruments of wickedness,[12] but rather as slaves of righteous-

---

6. *Forma*: see Phil 2:6 (Vg). Cf. chapter 14 below, in which the same idea and terminology recur.
7. Wis 8:1 (Vg).
8. See Ps 19:6; Eph 4:9.
9. "This passage is a little obscure," remarks W. Williams.
10. See 1 Cor 12:11.
11. See Rom 6:12.
12. See Rom 6:13.

ness.[13] And so, man will no longer be the slave of sin, since he does not commit sin.[14] Further, set free from sin, he can now begin to recover his freedom of counsel and vindicate his dignity, while setting up in himself a worthy likeness to the divine image, restoring, in fact, completely his former loveliness. But let him take care to do this no less gently than mightily, that is, not reluctantly or under compulsion[15]—for this is the beginning, not the fullness of wisdom—but with prompt and ready will, which makes the offering acceptable, since "God loves a cheerful giver."[16] In this way, in all he does, he will be imitating wisdom, mightily resisting vices and gently at rest within his conscience.

35. We cannot achieve these things, however, without the help of him by whose example we are spurred on to desire them. With it, and by it, we ourselves are conformed, and transformed into the same image from glory to glory, as by the Spirit of the Lord.[17] But if by the Spirit of the Lord, then hardly by free choice. Let no one imagine therefore that free choice is so called because it concerns itself with good and evil with equal power or facility. It was indeed able to fall of itself; but could rise up again only through the Spirit of the Lord. Otherwise, neither God nor the holy angels, (since they are so good that they cannot be also evil), nor the fallen angels (since they are so bad that they are no longer capable of being good) could be said to have freedom of choice. Not only that; but we, too, would lose it after the resurrection, when we shall be inseparably united, some with the good and others with the bad.

NEITHER GOD NOR THE DEVIL LACKS FREE CHOICE

Now neither God nor the devil lacks free choice, since the fact that the former cannot be evil is not due to shaky neces-

---

13. See Rom 6:18.
14. See Jn 8:34 and Rom 6:6.
15. See 2 Cor 9:7.
16. 2 Cor 9:7; cf. Prov 22:8 (LXX).
17. See 2 Cor 3:18 (Vg).

sity but to a steady willingness in good and a willing steadiness while the later's being unable to seek after the good is not due to any violent oppression from outside but his own obstinate willingness in evil and his willing obstinacy. Free choice, consequently, is so called because whether in good or in evil, it makes the will equally free, since no one should be or can be referred to as either good or bad unless he is a willing subject. That is why he may rightly be said to be equally open to good and to evil, because on either side he feels an equal freedom in willing though not an equal ease in choosing.

CHAPTER ELEVEN

NEITHER GRACE NOR TEMPTATION DETRACTS
FROM FREEDOM OF CHOICE

T HE CREATOR ENDOWED his rational creature, as we have said, with this prerogative of his divine dignity: that even as he himself was independent and master of his own will and hence not good by any necessity, so the creature, too, was made his own master to that extent that he would become evil only by his will and so justly be damned, or remain good by his will and deservedly be saved. Not that his will alone would be capable of gaining him salvation, but would never stand a chance of gaining it without his will. No one is unwillingly saved.

GOD JUDGES NO ONE WORTHY OF SALVATION
UNLESS HE FINDS HIM WANTING IT

For, what we read in the Gospel: "No one can come to me unless my Father draws him,"[1] and again elsewhere: "Compel people to come in,"[2] does not mean that, because the kindly Father who wills that all men be saved[3] appears as drawing and compelling many to salvation, this stands in the way of his judging worthy of salvation only such as he has previously proved to will it. Again, in frightening and in smiting men, his aim is not to save the unwilling, but rather to make them willing. In this way, changing their will from bad

1. See Jn 6:44.
2. Lk 14:23.
3. 1 Tim 2:4.

to good, he does not take away their freedom, but transfers its allegiance. Nevertheless, we have not always to be dragged along unwillingly; the blind or the weary seldom grumble at being helped along. Paul did not when he was lead by the hand to Damascus.[4] And that soul also willed to be drawn spiritually, who pleaded so earnestly for this in the Song of Songs: "Draw me after you," she said, "we will run in the odor of your ointments."[5]

37. The following texts, on the contrary all may be thought to force the will and undermine freedom: "Each person is tempted when he is lured and enticed by his own desire,"[6] and "A perishable body weighs down the soul, and this earthly tent burdens the thoughtful mind;"[7] and again those words of the Apostle: "I find in my members another law at war with the law of my mind and making me captive to the law of sin which dwells in my members."[8] Nevertheless, however much one may be assailed by temptation whether from within or from without, in regard to choice the will remains always itself and freely determines its own consent. With regard, on the other hand, to counsel and pleasure, it feels itself less free indeed, since the concupiscence of the flesh and the misery of life keep resisting; but it does not feel positively bad as long as it does not consent to the bad.

THE WORDS OF THE APOSTLE COMPLAINING
HE IS MADE A CAPTIVE OF SIN

Finally, Paul, who complains of being made captive to the law of sin—doubtless because he has not full freedom of counsel—yet glories in the health of his consent to good, seeing that in this he is still in large measure free: "It is no longer I," he says, "that do it."[9] What makes you so sure of that, Paul? Because, he says, "I agree that the law of God is good,"[10] and "I delight in the law of God, in my inmost self."[11] If only the eye is simple, then he presumes the whole

4. See Acts 9:8.
5. Song 1:4 (Vg).
6. Jas 1:14.
7. Wis 9:15.

8. Rom 7:23.
9. Rom 720.
10. Rom 7:16.
11. Rom 7:22.

body to be full of light.[12] The consent of his will being unimpaired, he does not hesitate to profess that, although drawn to sin and captive to sorrow, he is still free in well-doing. In this confidence it is that he draws the general conclusion: "There is therefore no condemnation for those who are in Christ Jesus."[13]

12. See Mt 6:22.
13. Rom 8:1.

CHAPTER TWELVE

WHETHER ONE WHO, FOR FEAR OF DEATH OR PUNISHMENT, DENIES THE FAITH, IS TO BE EXCUSED FROM BLAME, OR TO BE REGARDED AS DEPRIVED OF FREE CHOICE

B UT NOW LET US CONSIDER for a moment those who are forced, whether by the fear of death or of some penalty, to deny their faith, though in word only, and see whether, according to this statement, there was either no guilt (in that their denial was purely verbal) or else that the will itself could be forced into a state of guilt (so that a person could will what obviously he did not will and free choice would perish). Since this latter is impossible—namely, that a man should simultaneously will and not will the same thing—our question is: how is it that evil can be imputed to those who in no way will the evil? This case is not identical with that of original sin, where someone not yet baptised is constrained on other grounds, not only unwillingly but even, for the most part, unwittingly. The Apostle Peter may serve as an example. He appears to have denied the truth against his own will: it was a matter of deny or die.[1] Fearing death, he denied. He did not wish to deny, but still less did he wish to die. Thus, unwillingly sure enough, he denied, for fear of death. Now, though the man was compelled to say with his tongue, and not with his will, what he did not want to say, he did not nevertheless, will other than what he was accustomed to will. His tongue was moved against his will. But what of the will? Was that changed? What did he actually want? Undoubtedly, to be what he was, Christ's disciple. And what did he say? "I do not know the man."[2] Why did he say

1. See Mt 26:70.   2. Mt 26:72.

this? He wanted to escape death. What was wrong with
that?

THE WILL OF PETER WAS CULPABLE BECAUSE IT
CHOSE TO LIE RATHER THAN TO DIE

Here we have, therefore, two wills of the Apostle: the one,
quite innocent, by which he wished not to die; the other,
most praiseworthy, by which he rejoiced in the fact of being
a Christian. In what, then, was he to blame? Was it that he
preferred to lie rather than to die? Indeed this will of his was
reprehensible; it meant that he was more interested in saving
his body's life than his soul's: "A lying mouth destroys the
soul."[3] And so he sinned, not without the consent of his own
will either, weak and vapid indeed, but nonetheless free. He
sinned, not by hating or rejecting Christ, but by loving himself to excess. Nor did the fear of the moment force his will
into this perverse self-love; it proved it to exist. Without
doubt, he already was such a man as this, though without
being aware of it, when he heard from him to whom no
secret was veiled: "Before the cock crows, you will deny me
three times."[4] That weakness of will, unmasked, though not
caused, by sudden fear, brought it to light not to Christ but
to Peter; for Christ already "knew what was in man."[5] Insofar, therefore, as he loved Christ, that will of his undeniably
suffered violence to make it speak in spite of itself; but insofar as he loved himself, he freely consented to speak on his
own behalf. Had he not loved Christ, his denial would not
have been unwilling; but had he not loved himself even more,
there would not have been any denial. We must consequently
grant that the man was forced, if not to change, yet to dis-
semble his own will: forced, I say, not to recede from the
love of God, but somewhat to yield to love of self.

39. But does this imply that all our earlier assertion regarding the freedom of the will was mistaken, since we have
discovered that the will can be forced? Yes, if it could be
forced by some cause other than itself. If, however, it was

3. Wis 1:11.   4. Mt 26:34.

itself that did the forcing, being at once subjected and subjecting, then, just when it seemed to lose its freedom, it actually received it. For it was the first to generate the force to which it subjected itself.

PETER WAS NOT COMPELLED BUT BY HIS OWN WILL, CONSENTED IN SO FAR AS HE FEARED DEATH

Now, the fact that the will did generate this force means that it arose out of the will. But, if it was out of the will, then it was not necessary but voluntary. And, if voluntary, free. He then who was forced into denial by his own will, was forced because he willed it: or rather, he was not forced, but consented, not to any pressure from outside, but to his own will, to that will by which he wanted at all costs to avoid death. How otherwise would a woman's voice have been sufficient to tempt a holy tongue into pronouncing unholy words, had not the will, mistress of the tongue, assented? Finally, when later he came to control this excessive self-love and to love Christ as he ought to with his whole heart and soul and strength,[6] no threats or punishments could induce his will, however slightly, to yield its tongue as an instrument to sin,[7] but rather, courageously responding to the truth, he said: "We must obey God rather than men."[8]

THE TWOFOLD FORCE AGAINST FREE WILL: ACTIVE AND PASSIVE

40. There is, in fact, a twofold compulsion, by which we are forced either to do or to suffer something against our own will. Passive compusion (for that is what the first is rightly called) can sometimes occur without the voluntary consent of the sufferer but active compulsion never can. Consequently, evil which is brought about in us or relative to us is not imputable to us as long as we are unwilling. On the other hand, what is done by us is now not without fault on the part of the will. We are prevailed upon to will something

5. Jn 2:25.   7. See Rom 6:13.
6. See Mk 12:30.   8. Acts 5:29.

that would not happen did we not will it. There is thus also a certain active compulsion though this is inexcusable when it is voluntary. A Christian (let us say) was forced into denying Christ, sorrowfully, doubtless, yet willingly. He willed excessively to escape the threatening sword, and it was this will presiding within him which opened his mouth, not the sword he saw in front of him. The sword showed the will to be what it was; it did not force it. The will, not the sword, therefore, pushed the will into its guilty decision. As to those others whose will was healthy, they could be killed, but never made to yield. That is what had been foretold of them: "They shall do to you whatever they please";[9] to their limbs, that is, not to their hearts. It is not you who shall do whatever they please, it is they who do it; you shall suffer it. They shall torture your members, but have no effect on your will. They shall do their worst upon your flesh, but there will be nothing they can do about your soul.[10] Though the sufferer's body be in the power of the tormentor, the will is free. Their ferocity shall soon reveal if it is weak. If it is not, they shall not force it to be. Its weakness is its own, its health not its own, but from the Spirit of the Lord. And it is made healthy when it is renewed.

41. Now, renewal comes when, as the Apostle teaches, "beholding the glory of God, it is transformed into the same image from glory to glory (that is, from strength to strength) as by the Spirit of the Lord."[11]

FREE WILL STANDS BETWEEN FLESH AND SPIRIT

Between these two: the divine Spirit and the fleshly appetite, what is called in man free choice, or, in other words,

---

9. See Mk 9:13 par. (Vg: " . . . they did to him whatever they pleased.")

10. See Mt 10:28. For the passage, "That is what had been foretold of them . . . but there will be nothing they can do about your soul," certain other versions have: "That is what was said of John: They did to him whatever they pleased. Was it what *he* pleased? So they did with the other martyrs not what the martyrs pleased, but what they themselves pleased. They did to them, I say, what they pleased, but to their members, not to their hearts. They tortured their members, but failed to change their will. They did their worst upon their flesh, but were unable to do anything about their soul."

11. 2 Cor 3:18. For parenthesis, see Ps 84:7.

human will, occupies as it were a middle position. Able to go in either direction, it is, as it were, on the sloping side of a fairly steep mountain. It is so weakened in its desires by the flesh that only with the Spirit constantly helping its infirmity through grace[12] is it capable of righteousness (which, to quote the Prophet, is like the mountains of God[13]), capable of ascending from strength to strength right up to the summit. Without that help, borne by the pull of its own weight, it would tumble headlong down the precipice, from vice to vice. This pull would come not only from the law of sin originally implanted in its members, but from the habit of worldliness long implanted in its affections. Scripture recalls this twofold load on the human will in one short verse, when it says: "A perishable body weighs down the soul, and this earthly tent burdens the thoughtful mind."[14] And even as these two ills of our mortality do not injure, but test, those who do not consent, so neither do they excuse, but rather condemn, those who do. Thus there can be no salvation nor damnation without the previous consent of the will, lest freedom of choice might appear to be in any respect predetermined.

12. See Rom 8:26.
13. See Ps 36:6.
14. Wis 9:15.

CHAPTER THIRTEEN

HUMAN MERITS ARE GOD'S GIFTS

CONSEQUENTLY, that which in the creature is called free choice, is either justly condemned, since it is not preordained to sin by any external influence, or else is mercifully saved, an end it is quite incapable of achieving on its own. In all of this, however, the reader should remember that the idea of original sin is not being considered. For the rest, free choice must not seek the reason for its condemnation anywhere outside of itself, since its own fault alone condemns it; nor within itself the merit of its salvation, since mercy alone is responsible for saving it. Vain indeed, would be its efforts to do good were grace not at hand to help it; they would not even be, had they received no stimulus. Moreover, as Scripture observes, man's senses and thoughts are prone to evil.[1] Accordingly, as has been said, his merits must be seen as coming not from himself, but as descending from above, from the Father of lights,[2] provided only that those merits by which eternal salvation is gained be truly reckoned among the good endowments and perfect gifts.

GOD DIVIDED HIS GIFTS INTO MERITS AND GIFTS

43. For when God, our King from of old,[3] worked salvation in the midst of the earth,[4] he divided the gifts which he

1. See Gen 8:21.   3. See Ps 74:12.
2. See Jas 1:17.   4. Ibid.

gave to men into merits and rewards,[5] in order that, on the
one hand, our merits might be our own here and now by free
possession, and, on the other, by a gracious promise, we
might await their recompense as our due, in fact even long
for it, in the life to come. Paul draws attention to both these
aspects when he says: "The return you get is sanctification,
and its end, eternal life."[6] And again he says: "We ourselves,
who have the first fruits of the Spirit, groan inwardly as we
wait for adoption as sons,"[7] calling "sanctification" the first
fruits of the Spirit; that is, those virtues by which in our
present condition we are sanctified by the Spirit, in order
that we may deservedly attain to adoption. These same things
are once more promised in the Gospel to such as renounce
the world, when it says: "He will receive a hundredfold, and
inherit eternal life."[8] Hence, salvation is from the Lord,[9] not
from free choice. Indeed, he is both salvation and the way to
salvation, who said: "I am the salvation of the people,"[10] and
elsewhere: "I am the way."[11] He who was also salvation and
life made himself the way, so that no human being might
boast.[12] If, then, merits are the good things of the pilgrim's way
even as salvation and life are of the homeland, and if
David spoke truly when he said: "There is none that does

5. See Eph 4:8; cf. Ps 68:18.
6. Rom 6:22.
7. Rom 8:23.
8. Mt 19:29.
9. See Ps 3:8.
10. See Ps 35:3 (Vg. "I am your salvation.") Bernard, however, is not quoting
this psalm, but the Introit of the Mass for the nineteenth Sunday after Pentecost
in the old rite: "Salus populi ego sum, dicit Dominus...." In *Recueil d'Etudes
sur S. Bernard et ses Ecrits,* I, (Roma: Edizioni di Storia e Letteratura, 1962), p.
307, Jean Leclercq asks the surprising question: "Did Bernard read the Bible? " In
other words, when he quotes does he quote directly from a memory nourished
directly on Scripture, or perhaps indirectly only? He replies in a note to the
effect that Bernard was familiar with the books of the New Testament from
personal reading, but with the Old Testament—and notably certain parts of the
Wisdom literature—often through the liturgy. Bernard quotes this Introit again in
SC 15:8; CF 4:112.
11. Jn 14:6.
12. See 1 Cor 1:29.

good, except for one"[13]—that one, namely, of whom it is also
said: "No one is good but God alone"[14]—then both our
works and his rewards are undoubtedly God's gifts, and he
who placed himself in our debt by his gifts constituted us by
our works real deservers. To form a basis for such meriting he
deigns to make use of the ministry of creatures, not that he
stands in any need of it, but that through this or by its means
he may benefit them.

THE THREEFOLD OPERATION OF GOD THROUGH CREATURES: NAMELY, WITHOUT THEIR CONSENT, AGAINST THEIR CONSENT AND WITH THEIR CONSENT

44. He, therefore, accomplishes the salvation of those
whose names are in the book of life,[15] sometimes through the
creature yet without it, sometimes through the creature but
against it, and sometimes through the creature and with it.
Many a saving thing is rendered to man, in fact, by means of
an insensible or irrational creature, which, consequently, is
said to happen without it, since, lacking an intellect, it cannot act consciously. God also performs many things as a help
to the salvation of many, by means of wicked men or wicked
angels; but, since these latter are unwilling means, such divine
activity may be said to take place against them.[16] For lending
God a helping hand out of a desire to inflict injury, they hurt
themselves as much as this perverse intention as they profit
others by their useful action. Then there are those through
whom and with whom God works; such are the good angels
and men who both do and will whatever God wills. For God
truly communicates the work he carries out through them to
those who consent in will to what they do in act. Hence Paul,
in telling of the many good deeds God had wrought through

13. Ps 14:3. The Hebrew means (as RSV renders it): "There is none that does
good, no, not one." But Bernard interprets the Vg.

14. Lk 18:19.

15. See Phil 4:3.

16. W. Williams refers to the cases of Pharaoh (Exod 9:16; Rom 9:17), of
Balaam (Num 22:18; 24:13) and of the Chaldeans (Hab 1:6).

him, qualifies: "though it was not I, but the grace of God which is with me."[17] He might have said "through me," but, because that would have been too little, he preferred to say "with me," supposing himself to be not merely the minister of the work through its accomplishment, but in some way also the associate of the worker by his consent.

45. Let us see in respect to the threefold manner of God's working, as just stated, what the creature merits for its service. What, in fact, can an instrument merit, by means of which and without which something is effected? What else but wrath can that merit against which a thing is done? What but grace that with which it is done?

WHAT EACH CREATURE MERITS

In the first case, accordingly, no merits are won; in the next, only demerits; and in the last, true merits. For when something good or evil is done by means of animals, these merit neither weal or woe, since they have not the capacity to consent either way. Much less do the stones merit, since they lack even sense-perception. The devil, or a wicked man, on the other hand, rationally both alive and alert, earns something for his trouble; only punishment, however, for they dissent from the good. But Paul, who is wholeheartedly in his work of evangelizing, so as not to be acting as a mere mercenary,[18] and anyone who follows his example, may rest assured that there is laid up for them a crown of righteousness[19] because they obeyed by the consent of their will. With an eye to man's salvation, God makes use, then, of irrational and even insensible creatures, as a pack-animal or tool which, their work done, are put aside. He uses rational but malevolent creatures after the manner of a switch which, once em-

17. 1 Cor 15:10.
18. See 1 Cor 9:16f. What Bernard is saying is that Paul's apostolic labor is meritorious in that he does it not as a hired workman working for pay, and hence by contract obligation, but *volens,* willingly, gladly, and without undue concern for remuneration.
19. See 2 Tim 4:8.

ployed on his son, he throws into the fire as a useless twig.[20]
He uses angels and men of good will, as his allies and com-
rades-in-arms whom, at the hour of victory, he will most
amply reward. To quote Paul again, boldly referring to himself and his imitators: "We are God's fellow-workers."[21] God,
therefore, kindly gives man the credit, as often as he deigns
to perform some good act through him and with him. That is
why we presume to apply to ourselves the titles of "God's
fellow-workers," co-operators with the Holy Spirit, meriters
of the kingdom, in that we have become united with the
divine will by our own voluntary consent.

20. See Jn 15:6.
21. 1 Cor 3:9.

CHAPTER FOURTEEN

WHAT PART IS TO BE ASSIGNED TO GRACE, AND WHAT TO FREE CHOICE IN THE WORK OF SALVATION

ARE WE TO SAY, then, that the entire function and the sole merit of free choice lie in its consent? Assuredly. Not that this consent, in which all merit consists, is its own doing, since we are unable even to think anything of ourselves;[1] which is less than to consent.

GOOD THOUGHT IS FROM GOD, CONSENT AND ACT ALSO ARE FROM HIM BUT NOT WITHOUT US

These words are not mine but the Apostle's, who attributes to God and not to his own choosing power, everything susceptible of good: thinking, willing, and accomplishing for his good pleasure.[2] If, then, God works these three things in us, namely thinking, willing and accomplishing the good, the first he does without us; the second, with us; and the third, through us. By suggesting the good thought, he goes one first step ahead of us; by also bringing about the change of our ill will, he joins it to himself by its consent; and by supplying consent with faculty and ability, the operator within makes his appearance outwardly through the external work that we perform. Of ourselves, we cannot, of course, take that first step. But he who can find no one who is good, can save no one without himself first stepping into the lead. There can be

1. See 2 Cor 3:5.
2. See Phil 2:13.

no doubt, therefore, that the beginning of our salvation rests with God, and is enacted neither through us nor with us. The consent and the work, however, though not originating from us, nevertheless are not without us.

NEITHER CONSENT NOR THE ACT ARE ACCOMPLISHED WITHOUT GOOD WILL

So neither the first, since we are in no way involved in it; nor the last, which results, more often than not, from useless fear or damnable hypocrisy; but only the second, redounds to our merit. Good will suffices on its own at times; if it is wanting, everything else is of no avail. Of no avail to the agent, that is, but not to the beholder. Thus, intention is capable of merit; action of giving example; and the good thought preceding both, only of arousing from inertia.

47. We must therefore be careful, whenever we feel these things happening invisibly within us and with us, not to attribute them to our own will, which is weak; nor to any necessity on the part of God, for there is none; but to that grace alone of which he is full. This it is which arouses free choice, when it sows the seed of the good thought; which heals it, by changing its disposition; which strengthens it, so as to lead it to action; which saves it from experiencing a fall. It so cooperates with free choice, however, that only in the first case does it go a step ahead of it; in the others, it accompanies it. Indeed, its whole aim in taking the step ahead is that from then on it may co-operate with it. What was begun by grace alone, is completed by grace and free choice together, in such a way that they contribute to each new achievement not singly but jointly; not by turns, but simultaneously. It is not as if grace did one half of the work and free choice the other; but each does the whole work, according to its own peculiar contribution. Grace does the whole work, and so does free choice—with this one qualification: that whereas the whole is done *in* free choice, so is the whole done *of* grace.

48. We trust the reader may be pleased to find that we have never strayed far from the Apostle's meaning, and that wherever our words may wander, we find ourselves often return-

ing to almost his very words. For what else does what we are saying amount to but: "So it depends not upon man's will or exertion, but God's mercy?"[3] He does not say this as if it were possible for a person to will or to run in vain;[4] what he means is that the man who wills and runs would glory not in himself, but in him from whom he received in the first place the power both to will and to run. In a word: "What have you that you did not receive?"[5]

THE THREEFOLD OPERATION OF GOD: CREATION, FORMATION, CONSUMMATION

You are created, healed, saved. Which of these, O man, comes from you? Which is not impossible to free choice? You could neither create yourself, since you were not there to do so; nor, when in sin, could you restore yourself to grace; nor raise yourself from the dead, to say nothing of those other good things,[6] which are either necessary to those who have to be healed, or laid up in store for those who are to be saved. This is obvious enough in the case of creation and salvation. Yet, no one doubts it even in regard to justification except the man who, being ignorant of the righteousness that comes from God and seeking to establish his own, does not submit himself to God's righteousness.[7] For can it be that, while acknowledging the power of the Creator and the glory of the Savior, you are ignorant of the righteousness of the Healer? "Heal me," said the Prophet, "and I shall be healed; save me, and I shall be saved; for you are my praise."[8] He acknowledged the righteousness of God, and hoped at the same time both to be healed of his sin by him and to be cut free from sorrow. Hence he rightly declared that God, not himself, was his praise. For this reason also, David cried out: "Not to us, O Lord, not to us, but to your name give glory";[9] for it was from God that he was looking

3. Rom 9:16.
4. See Gal 2:2.
5. 1 Cor 4:7.
6. See 1 Cor 2:9.
7. See Rom 10:3.
8. Jer 17:14.
9. Ps 115:1.

for both robes, that is to say, the robe of righteousness and the robe of glory.[10]

THE SELF-RIGHTEOUS MAN DOES NOT
KNOW THE RIGHTEOUSNESS OF GOD

Who is unaware of God's righteousness? The self-righteous man. And who is he? The man who imagines that his merits come from some source other than from grace. Further, it is the one who made what he would save who also provides the means of salvation. He, I mean, bestows the merits, who in the first place made those on whom he would bestow them. "What shall I give back to the Lord," he says, "for all that he has (he does not say *given* but) *given back* to me?"[11] He proclaims that being and righteousness alike he has from God, lest, were he to deny either, he might lose both: separating himself from the source of his righteousness and so condemning his being.[12] But now, in the third place, he finds that which in his turn he should repay: "I will take," he says, "the cup of salvation."[13] This cup of salvation is the Savior's blood. Hence, if you lack anything you can call your own, which you might give back even for the second gift of God to you, from what source do you promise yourself salvation? "I will call," he says, "on the name of the Lord,"[14] that name upon which, whoever calls shall be saved.[15]

49. Those, therefore, who are possessed of true wisdom, acknowledge a threefold operation, not indeed of free choice, but of divine grace in, or concerning, free choice. The first is creation; the second, reformation; and the third, consummation. Created first in Christ[16] unto freedom of will, by the

10. For the "robe of glory," see Sir 45:7 and 5:11. The "robe of righteousness" is possibly a reference to Is 61:10, Bar 5:2 or Eph 6:14. Otherwise it does not occur in the Vg.
11. Ps 116:12.
12. "His self-righteousness," explains W. Williams, "would deprive him of grace, and the loss of grace would mean the death of his soul."
13. Ps 116:13.
14. Ibid.
15. See Acts 2:21; 3:12.
16. See Eph 2:10.

second we are reformed through Christ unto the spirit of freedom,[17] lastly to reach fulfillment with Christ unto the state of eternity. It had to be, in fact, that what had no existence should be created by one who had; that what was deformed should be reformed through the Form; that the members should be perfected in no other way than with the head. This will happen when we all shall have attained "to mature manhood, to the measure of the stature of the fullness of Christ,"[18] when Christ who is our life, appearing, we also shall appear with him in glory.[19] Seeing, then, that fulfillment takes place in relation to us, or even in us, but not by us; whereas creation happens also without us; reformation alone, occuring as it does to some extent with us on account of our voluntary consent, will be reckoned for us as merit.

INTENTION–AFFECTION–MEMORY

These merits are our fasting, watchings, continence, works of mercy and other virtuous practices, by means of which, as is evident, our inner nature is renewed every day.[20] Our intention, bent down under the weight of earthly cares, rises again slowly from depths to heights; the affection, languishing in fleshly desires, gradually gains strength for spiritual love; and our memory, sullied by the shame of former deeds, but now become clean once more with continual good works, reaches each day a new measure of joy.[21] In these three things it is that interior renewal consists: rightness of intention, purity of affection, and the remembrance of good work, this last leading the memory, in full self-awareness, to shed its light about it.

17. See 2 Cor 3:17f.
18. Eph 4:13.
19. See Col 3:4.
20. See 2 Cor 4:16.
21. Though Bernard adopts Augustine's division of the soul into memory, reason, and will, he nevertheless understands "memory" in its commonly accepted sense of remembering faculty, and not as Augustine understood it. See E. von Ivanka's essay, "La Structure de l'Ame selon S. Bernard," *S. Bernard Théologien*, (above, note 13). Also Venuta, *Libero Arbitrio e Libertà della Grazia*, p. 44, note 1.

50. Since it is clearly the divine Spirit who activates these things in us, they are God's gifts; yet because they come about by the assent of our will, they are our merits. "For it is not you who speak," he says, "but the Spirit of your Father speaking through you."[22] And the Apostle: "Do you desire proof that Christ is speaking in me? "[23] If Christ, then, or the Holy Spirit is speaking in Paul, is he not also at work in him? "For I will not venture to speak," he says, "of anything except what Christ has wrought through me."[24] But what does this mean? If, since the words and works of the one speaking or working through Paul are not Paul's but God's where are Paul's merits? And what becomes of those confident words of his: "I have fought the good fight, I have finished the race, I have kept the faith. Henceforth there is laid up for me the crown of righteousness, which the Lord, the righteous judge, will award to me on that Day"? [25] Did he perhaps think that a crown would be laid up for him because these things were wrought through him? But then many good things happen by means of the wicked, whether they be angels or men, without their being reckoned for them as merits. Or was it not rather that they were done with his co-operation, that is, with his good will? "For," said he, "if I preach the gospel unwillingly, I am entrusted with a commission; but if I do it willingly it is to my glory."[26]

51. There is another question: if not even so much as the will, on which all merit depends, is from Paul himself, how can he refer to the crown, which he presumes is laid up for him, as a crown of righteousness? Is it that one can justly demand as a debt whatever is promised gratis? [27]

22. Mt 10:20.
23. 2 Cor 13:3.
24. Rom 15:18.
25. 2 Tim 4:7f.
26. See 1 Cor 9:16f.
27. The answer, of course, is "yes." On the important and encouraging New Testament idea of God's "steadfastness" or "faithfulness" (*pistotes*), see 1 Cor 1:9; 10:13; 2 Cor 1:18; 1 Thess 5:24; 2 Thess 3:3; Heb 10:23; 11:11; 2 Tim 2:13; 1 Jn 1:9; 1 Pet 4:19.

THE CROWN PAUL EXPECTS IS THE CROWN OF
GOD'S RIGHTEOUSNESS, NOT HIS OWN

He says: "I know in whom I have believed, and I am sure that he is able to guard what has been entrusted to me."[28] He calls the promise of God something that has been entrusted to him. Because he believed the one promising, with confidence he repeats the promise, which, arising out of mercy, must be fulfilled out of justice. Hence, the crown Paul awaits is a crown of righteousness, but of God's righteousness, not his own. It is only just that he should deliver what he owes; and he owes what he promised. This is the righteousness Paul is relying on, the promise of God, lest, in any way despising it, and seeking to establish his own, he might be failing to submit to God's righteousness.[29] God, however, wished to have him as partaker of his righteousness in order that he might also make him deserving of a crown. For he made him partaker of his righteousness and deserving of a crown when he deigned to choose him as his fellow-worker in the works to which the promise of the crown was attached. But he chose him as his fellow-worker when he made him a willing person, or, in other words, a consenter to his will. Thus, while the will is given in view of helping, the helping is reckoned as merit. If, therefore, the willing is from God, so too is the merit. Nor can it be doubted that it belongs to God "both to will and to work for his good pleasure."[30] God is, in consequence, the author of merit, who both applies the will to the work, and supplies the work to the will. Besides, if the merits which we refer to as ours are rightly so called, then they are seed-beds of hope, incentives to love, portents of a hidden predestination, harbingers of happiness, the road to the kingdom, not a motive for playing the king. In one word: it is those whom he made righteous, not those whom he found already righteous, that he has magnified.[31]

28. 2 Tim 1:12.
29. See Rom 10:3.

30. Phil 2:13.
31. See Rom 8:30.

IN PRAISE OF THE NEW KNIGHTHOOD

INTRODUCTION

IN THE YEAR 1129 or thereabouts an English clerk by name of Philip from the diocese of Lincoln set out on a pilgrimage to the Holy Land. On his way to Jerusalem he stopped at Clairvaux. Shortly afterwards the Bishop of Lincoln received a letter from the Abbot of Clairvaux, announcing the good tidings that Philip had arrived safely and very quickly at his destination, and that he intended to remain there permanently. "He has entered the holy city and has chosen his heritage. . . . He is no longer an inquisitive onlooker but a devout inhabitant and an enrolled citizen of Jerusalem." But this Jerusalem, "if you want to know, is Clairvaux. She is the Jerusalem united to the one in heaven by whole-hearted devotion, by conformity of life and by a certain spiritual affinity."[1]

The true home of the Christian—according to the medieval conception—is the heavenly Jerusalem. Not that he must despise the terrestrial Jerusalem, but the true terrestrial Jerusalem which is "united to the one in heaven" is there where the perfect Christian life is lived. We recognize in this letter the voice of the same Abbot of Clairvaux who refused the offer, in 1131, by the Crusader King of Jerusalem, Baldwin II, of the site of St Samuel (also known as Mountjoy or Mons Gaudii) northwest of Jerusalem, encouraging the Premonstra-

---

1. Ep 64, PL 182:169-170; Bruno Scott James, *The Letters of St. Bernard of Clairvaux* (London: Burns Oates, 1953) hereafter cited as LBJ, Ep 67, pp. 90-92.

tensians to establish themselves there instead of the Cistercians.[2] Yet the same Bernard also preached the Second Crusade and helped to establish the "new knighthood" that consecrated itself to the protection of pilgrims in the Holy Land. In order to understand St Bernard's views on these and related subjects it is necessary, first and foremost, to avoid undue simplification.

For many centuries Christianity had been caught between the horns of the dilemma of the heavenly *versus* the earthly Jerusalem. Piety and a devout reverence for the sites associated with the earthly ministry of Christ had always stimulated pilgrimages to the land and to the places where the divine act of salvation, for all its universal—and, according to many early Christian writers, even cosmic-significance, had had its local habitation and incarnate manifestation. At the same time there were also voices warning against pilgrimages, casting doubt on their value (e.g., St Gregory of Nyssa[3]) and suggesting that this practice was not always or necessarily conducive to sanctification (e.g., the author of *The Imitation of Christ*). Commenting on the words of Jesus "if any man thirst, let him come unto me and drink" (Jn 7:37), St Augustine wrote:

> When we thirst, then we should come—not with our feet but rather with our feelings; we should come not by wandering but by loving. In an inward way to love is to wander. It is one thing to wander with the body, and a different thing to wander with the heart. He who wanders with the body changes his place by the motion of the body; he who wanders with the heart changes his feelings by the motion of the heart.[4]

2. See the letter of St Bernard to Abbot Hugh of Prémontré; LBJ, EP 328, p. 404.

3. Cf. the letter in PG 46:1009-1013 and especially the exhortation (*ibid.,* col 1013) "advise therefore the brethren to ascend from the body to God rather than from Cappadocia to Palestine." Since the aforementioned Philip meant to go from England to Jerusalem it may be apposite to refer also to St Jerome, Ep 58 (PL 22:579-586) and his statement (*ibid.,* col. 581) *et de Jerosolymis et de Britania patet aula coelestis, Regnum enim Dei intra vos est.*

4. *In Joannis Evangelium,* Tract. XXXII, PL 35:1642.

Yet by and large Christian piety has acted on the assumption that the movement of the body and that of the heart were not incompatible and that, on the contrary, the former could stimulate and promote the latter. Nevertheless, there is no simple rule-of-thumb formula that can be indiscriminately applied to all. As there are varieties of gifts so there are varieties of vocations, and St Bernard held very strong views as regards the specific practical and spiritual implications of the several vocations. Pilgrimages may be useful to a certain kind of Christian; they are not necessarily so to them that have already "entered the holy city" of the monastic life. The man that fired Europe with enthusiasm for the Second Crusade also demanded that monks who left the monastery to take the cross be excommunicated. "Why do they sew the sign of the Cross on their shoulders, when they always carry it on their hearts? "[5] Even when congratulating Hugh, the Count of Champagne, for becoming a knight of the Temple, St Bernard does not hide his regret that the Count had not preferred to become a monk at Clairvaux.[6]

The knights of the Temple were a group of men who meant to sew the sign of the Cross on their shoulders whilst always carrying it in their hearts. In fact, when Hugh de Payens decided to found his "new knighthood" it was obvious that he initiated something utterly new. By taking the vows of poverty, chastity, and obedience, the Templars undertook to sanctify the idea of knighthood—and St Bernard leaves us in no doubt as to what he thought of contemporary secular chivalry[7]—even as by taking arms this newly constituted religious order seemed to establish and institutionalize an irreconcilable contradiction. It is not without reason that Watkin Williams considered St Bernard's *In Praise of the New Knighthood* to be not so much a eulogy as essentially an "apology" —an authoritative apology for an unheard of and utterly new modality of the religious life.[8] St Bernard's justification

---

5. Letter to his Brother Abbots, LBJ, Ep 396, pp. 468-9.
6. Letter to Hugh; LBJ, Ep 32, p. 65.
7. See Text, c. 3, p. 00.
8. Watkin Williams, *Saint Bernard of Clairvaux* (Manchester, 1935), p. 238.

of the new order is another example of his capacity to differentiate varieties of vocations and their moral corollaries, and it may perhaps be useful to try and summarize briefly the main lines of his thinking on this particular subject.[9]

For it would be totally wrong to use this short treatise as a sourcebook for St Bernard's "theology of warfare."[10] Warfare is a grave problem to every conscience, and St Bernard's views on it would have to be pieced together from his utterances on the subject on many different occasions and in diverse contexts. St Bernard was first and foremost a man of peace and a maker of peace. Yet he certainly was no "pacifist" since he firmly believed that in many cases war, with all its attendant violence and bloodshed, was the lesser evil. He would certainly insist that war against Christians was a different matter from war against unbelievers. Christians today may hold different views on this subject—not only because views on war are changing but also because (especially after Vatican II) ideas about other religions and about "unbelievers" are being re-examined. In fact, the definition of "unbeliever" is becoming a major theological concern to the extent that traditional concepts such as "implicit faith" and the like are taken more seriously and are being vigorously rethought. Similarly, it is probably fair to say that modern Christian theology no longer holds the Jews to be simply the type of blind unbelief,[11] and surely there are better—and more Christian—reasons for condemning their persecution than those advanced by St Bernard in his letter to the clergy and people of eastern France and Bavaria.[12] Even so, St Ber-

9. Cf. Joshua Prawer's excellent characterization of St Bernard as a theologian: "Bernard of Clairvaux was no theologian in the traditional sense of the term, neither was he a specialist in Canon Law. Yet he could deal with the most acute theological issues of his time. He was, first and foremost, a man of burning faith whose writing and speaking was essentially preaching. His thinking was not always rigorously organised, and at times it is difficult to sort out the sequence of his ideas. But there can never be any possible doubt about his intentions."–J. Prawer, *Histoire du royaume latin de Jérusalem* (Paris, 1969), 1:348.

10. Cf. on this subject the note in *Bernard de Clairvaux,* Commission d'Histoire de l'Ordre de Cîtaux 3 (Dijon, 1953), p. 673.

11. See Text, p. 00.

12. Ep 363; for an identical letter addressed to the clergy and people of England, see LBJ, Ep 391, pp. 460-3. On St Bernard's efforts to save the Jews from massacres during the crusade, see also Prawer, *Histoire du royaume,* p. 351f.

nard was much in advance of his times when he insisted that pagans were not to be killed except for the protection of Christians against actual physical or moral danger.[13] There is war against heretics and schismatics, which Bernard sometimes encourages,[14] and there is frivolous fighting, such as the knightly tournaments which he unconditionally condemns as one of the most objectionable manifestations of chivalry.[15] What renders the fighting life of the new knighthood different from, and more problematic than, ordinary warfare is the fact that, as a religious vocation, it is voluntarily chosen— like the monastic life. St Bernard does not doubt that there are Christian soldiers "so destined by God," and that they are permitted to wield the sword.[16] But the *miles* as soldier is not quite the same as the *miles* as knight.[17] In his "Praise of the New Knighthood" St Bernard is concerned no less with the theology of a reformed and sanctified knighthood as with the theology of warfare.

Watkin Williams observed that if the Templars were a religious order, then it was because St Bernard was their "first novice-master."[18] This may be overstating the case a little. An impulsive and generous nature, St Bernard often entertained higher hopes of human nature than it deserved, and he consequently came to grief.[19] The end of his life was clouded by the failure of the Second Crusade. Bernard himself never doubted the righteousness of the cause or its conformity to God's will. But as a *Christian* undertaking, it was bound to fail if its protagonists were not *Christian* enough. We can

13. See text, no. 4, p. 00.
14. Cf. the letters to Henry I of England (LBJ, Ep 141, p. 209) and to the Emperor Lothair (LBJ, Ep 142, p. 210).
15. Letter to Abbot Suger (LBJ, pp. 476-7).
16. See text, no. 5, p. 00.
17. The semantic history of the words *miles* and *militia* is an interesting subject that cannot be pursued here. In early Christian history, the Christian *miles* was a soldier in the Roman army. In due course the word became invested with a spiritual meaning as shown by A. von Harnack, *Militia Christi* (1905) In the Middle Ages the *miles* became a knight. In later Latin the word again signified any fighter or soldier (and not specifically a knight) but this connotation could also be given a purely spiritual sense (as e.g. in Erasmus' *Enchiridion militis christiani*).
18. *Saint Bernard of Clairvaux*, p. 240.
19. Cf. also the remarks in J. Calmette et H. David, *Saint Bernard* (1953), p. 221.

detect something of this disillusionment in the aforementioned letter to Abbot Suger in which Bernard protests
against the intention of two returned crusaders, Henry son of
the Count of Champagne, and Robert de Dreux, the king's
brother, to hold a knightly tournament: "With what sort of
dispositions must they have taken the road to Jerusalem
when they return in this frame of mind! " St Bernard was
under no illusions as to what kind of men the new order
would attract: "former impious rogues, sacrilegious thieves,
murderers, perjurers and adulterers,"[20] but he rejoiced in this
"flood stream bringing glory to the nations" because he saw
in the throng of "faithful defenders" of the Holy Land a host
of penitents. We need not inquire here whether the charges
that ultimately led to the suppression of the order were justified or not. It is not impossible that—precisely as in the case
of the crusaders—the conversion was not sufficiently genuine,
sufficiently profound and sufficiently stable. When preaching
the Crusade, St Bernard depicted it as an act of grace and
mercy by which God offered "murderers, thieves, adulterers,
perjurers and such like" a chance to "find righteousness in his
service."

It is therefore with very good reason that Prof. J. Prawer,
of the Hebrew University of Jerusalem, in his standard work
on the Latin Kingdom of Jerusalem, entitles his chapter on
the Second Crusade: *Croisade du salut des âmes.*[21] Prawer
rightly insists that St Bernard's views on the Crusade and his
De Laude are of a piece and have to be considered together.
His works on this subject deserve to be quoted here in full:

> The new knight fights for the sake of the salvation of his
> soul and the love of his Creator. His supreme virtue and
> essential quality is his vocation for martyrdom: in fact, he
> is a permanent candidate for martyrdom. Martyrdom is the
> supreme goal of the knight's life. The Order of the Temple
> is the collectivity of knights dedicated to martyrdom.
> This conception brought Bernard close to the idea of the
> crusade, and indeed of the Holy Land as well. But in the

20. See text, no. 10, p. 00.
21. See Prawer, *Histoire du royaume* especially the pages on St Bernard, p.
348ff.

thinking of this monk, permeated by an ardent and almost
ecstatic faith, the real and historical purpose of the expedition almost disappeared. It was not the end but the means
chosen for its achievement that really mattered. The Crusade of Bernard of Clairvaux, a crusade for the salvation of
souls, sought neither revenge on Islam, nor a balance of
power at the frontiers of the Christian and the Muslim
world, nor the consolidation of the Latin state. It was an
expedition placed under the sign of the Cross and meant to
save the souls of the faithful. As a mater of fact the faithful, i.e. the good Christians, did not need it at all, for the
grace of God shows itself in them by the strength of their
faith and love, by their detachment from the life of this
world, and by the offering of their whole life under the sign
of the Cross. It was to the sinners . . . that a compassionate
and merciful God in his boundless love offered a path to
salvation commensurate to their abilities: the crusade. . . .
It was not the physical participation that mattered but the
spiritual preparation consisting in contrition and repentance.[22]

Alas, it is not always the righteousness of God that men seek
even when they appear to obey his voice. It did not occur to
St Bernard when he preached the Crusade that the murderers
might remain murderers, and the impious rogues—impious
rogues.

Less than half of this little tract is devoted to the actual
praise of the new knighthood. A considerable part of the text
is an allegorical meditation on the major holy places which
the knights are to protect and near which they shall have the
privilege to live. Notwithstanding the primacy of the spiritual
meaning of the holy geography of Palestine in general, and of
Jerusalem in particular, St Bernard's style waxes rhapsodic in
his evocations of the earthly Jerusalem as the *civitas Dei,* of
Zion "the city of our strength," and of the "sanctuary of
God." The allegorical meditation which St Bernard proposes
to the Knights of the Temple is not without theological interest and deserves a fuller analysis than can be accorded it here.

22. Prawer, pp. 349-350.

Chapter 21 ff.[23] are a kind of theological apologetic, justi-
fying the rationale and efficacy of salvation through Christ.
Why precisely this type of argument to this particular audi-
ence in this particular context? St Bernard's précis of the
doctrine of salvation at one point touches on a problem that
had stimulated one of St Anselm's major contributions to
medieval theology. Justice is as essentially an attribute of
God as is mercy. How is it possible to formulate a theology
of salvation by mercy that does not detract from God's justice? St Anselm grappled with the problem in his *Cur Deus
Homo.* St Bernard refers to the same issue in chs. 22-23 of
our text, and is at pains to show that while Christ's sacrifice
"is not justice, but mercy," its result, even though it "is not
justice, neither is it contrary to justice," for otherwise God
would not "at the same time be both just and merciful."[24]

The long theological excursus is presented in the form of a
meditation on the Holy Sepulchre.[25] The length of this meditation stands in marked contrast to the short paragraphs devoted to Bethlehem, Nazareth, the Mount of Olives, the Jordan, Mount Calvary, and Bethpage. Here St Bernard shows
himself very much in the western tradition. His central theme
is not the mystery of the Incarnation but that of salvation
through the death of Christ. This latter mystery is associated
not so much with Calvary as with the Sepulchre. A writer in
the eastern tradition would no doubt have given greater
prominence to the theme of the resurrection (which in our
text appears as a secondary motif only) rather than to that of
Christ's burial. However that may be, St Bernard's text can
be read with profit not only by students of the middle ages,
but by Christians thinking seriously about the anguishing and
ever present problem of the kind of murder that is called
warfare, as well as by pilgrims to the Holy Land, facing in the
most concrete and tangible manner the tension between eternal hope and actual history or—to use St Bernard's own

23. See text, p. 00.
24. See text, no. 23, p. 00.
25. See text, c. 11, pp. 00-00.

words—between "the spiritual meaning" of the biblical texts and "the temporal realizations of prophetic utterance."

R. J. Zwi Werblowsky

TRANSLATOR'S NOTE

What were St Bernard's motives in refusing the various opportunities he might have seized for establishing a Cistercian house in the Holy Land? We might dismiss his refusal of Mountjoy[1] with the old saying, "Benedictus montes amabat, Bernardus valles," but what about the project of Arnold of Morimond and his disciple Conrad of Bavaria?[2] Doubtless Bernard felt that the unstable political situation was an important factor: "It is evident that what is needed there are soldiers to fight rather than monks to pray",[3] but I suspect that the deciding reason was the distance and the difficulty of communication with the central government of the Order.[4] At any rate the sons of St Bernard waited over 700 years to realize this project. When they did come they settled in the smiling valley of Ayallon—where Josue made the sun stand still, and where the same sun still smiles on the richest vineyards in the East.

On the hill overlooking the monastery stand the ruins of a thirteenth-century crusader's castle, built by the same Templars for whom this treatise was written; and a half mile or so up the valley is Emmaus, where Christ broke bread with his disciples on the evening of the first Easter.

1. Bernard, Ep 355; PL 182:337; LBJ, Ep 275, p. 348; and Ep 253; PL 182:453; LBJ, Ep 328, p. 404. See also Vita Bern 3:22; PL 185:316.
2. Ep 4: PL 182:89; LBJ, Ep 4, pp. 20-22; and Ep 6; PL 182:92-93; LBJ, Ep 7, pp. 25-26.
3. Ep 359; PL 182:561; LBJ, Ep 5, pp. 23-24.
4. Ep 175; PL 182:337; LBJ, Ep 216, 294; and Ep 75; PL 182:189; LBJ, Ep 78; pp. 108-109.

Such is the setting in which Providence willed that this translation should be made. The work has been a real pleasure, as this is one of Bernard's better polished literary productions. The guide lines and general principles of this translation are the same as for the other treatises in this series, so there is no point in repeating here what has been said on that subject in previous translator's notes.

As a pioneer in amical judeo-christian relations, St Bernard must certainly be pleased with the scholarly introduction which Dean Zwi Werblowsky of the Hebrew University of Jerusalem has so kindly contributed. Few Jews (and for that matter, few Christians) would have been able to perform such a service, for which I thank him from the bottom of my heart.

May the earthly Jerusalem which Bernard never saw, but on whose soil his sons and successors are privileged to tread, continue to be the figure which prepares the glory of the heavenly Jerusalem, our mother! [5]

M. Conrad Greenia OCSO

Latroun, Israel

5. See text, no. 6, p. 00.

PROLOGUE

TO HUGH, KNIGHT OF CHRIST[1] AND MASTER OF CHRIST'S MILITIA:
BERNARD, IN NAME ONLY, ABBOT OF CLAIRVAUS, WISHES THAT
HE MIGHT FIGHT THE GOOD FIGHT[2]

I F I AM NOT MISTAKEN, MY DEAR HUGH, you
have asked me not once or twice, but three times to write
a few words of exhortation for you and your comrades.[3]
You say that if I am not permitted to wield the lance, at least
I might direct my pen against the tyrannical foe, and that this
moral, rather than material support of mine will be of no
small help to you.[4] I have put you off now for quite some
time, not that I disdain your request, but rather lest I be
blamed for taking it lightly and hastily. I feared I might
botch a task which could be better done by a more qualified

1. 2 Tim 2:3. The usual translation of *miles* is soldier, but in medieval Latin it
came to mean, at least for a time, knight. Hugh of Payens or Payns was according
to J. Richard ("Le milieu familial" in *Bernard de Clairvaux*, Commission d'Histoire de l'Ordre de Cîteaux [Paris: Alsatia, 1953], pp. 13-14) a relative of Saint
Bernard. He started the Knights of the Temple in 1118 with eight companions
and was their Grand Master until his death in 1136.
2. 2 Tim 4:7.
3. In "Un document sur les débuts des Templiers" in *Revue d'histoire ecclésias-
tique* 52 (1957), pp. 81-91, Jean Leclercq edits a letter which he urges as being
written by Hugh of Payens and giving the background for this exhortation and
defense on the part of Saint Bernard. However, C. Sclafert in his "Lettre inédite
de Hughes de Saint-Victor aux chevaliers du Temple" in *Revue d'ascetique et de
mystique* 34 (1958), pp. 275-299, gives cogent arguments for attributing the
letter to Hugh of St Victor. Leclercq republished his article, unchanged, in *Recueil d'études sur saint Bernard et ses écrits II* (Rome: Edizioni di Storia e
Letteratura, 1966), pp. 87-99, adding at the end a "Post-scriptum" in which he
notes Fr Sclafert's article and concludes: " ... l'attribution à Hugues de Saint-
Victor est les plus vraisemblable." (p. 99).
4. Leclercq sees in the imagery Bernard uses here an indication that he is writing
a defence, *art. cit., Recueil*, p. 98.

hand, and which would perhaps remain, because of me, just as necessary and all the more difficult.

Having waited thus for quite some time to no purpose, I have now done what I could, lest my inability should be mistaken for unwillingness. It is for the reader to judge the result. If some perhaps find my work unsatisfactory or short of the mark, I shall be nonetheless content, since I have not failed to give you my best.

CHAPTER ONE

A WORD OF EXHORTATION FOR THE KNIGHTS OF THE TEMPLE

IT SEEMS THAT A NEW KNIGHTHOOD has recently appeared on the earth, and precisely in that part of it which the Orient from on high visited in the flesh.[1] As he then troubled the princes of darkness in the strength of his mighty hand,[2] so there he now wipes out their followers, the children of disbelief,[3] scattering them by the hands of his mighty ones.[4] Even now he brings about the redemption of his people[5] raising up again a horn of salvation for us in the house of his servant David.[6]

This is, I say, a new kind of knighthood and one unknown to the ages gone by. It ceaselessly wages a twofold war both against flesh and blood and against a spiritual army of evil in the heavens.[7] When someone strongly resists a foe in the flesh, relying solely on the strength of the flesh, I would hardly remark it, since this is common enough. And when war is waged by spiritual strength against vices or demons, this, too, is nothing remarkable, praiseworthy as it is, for the world is full of monks.[8] But when the one sees a man power-

---

1. Lk 1:78. This was indeed a new knighthood, the idea of men consecrated by religious vows bearing arms was utterly novel.

2. Eph 6:12; Is 10:13.

3. Eph 2:2.

4. Nahum 2:5.

5. Lk 1:68.

6. Lk 1:69.

7. Eph 6:12.

8. This may have been true of the Europe of St Bernard, but it was perhaps more remarkable than he realized.

fully girding himself[9] with both swords[10] and nobly marking his belt,[11] who would not consider it worthy of all wonder, the more so since it has been hitherto unknown? He is truly a fearless knight and secure on every side, for his soul is protected by the armor of faith[12] just as his body is protected by armor of steel. He is thus doubly armed and need fear neither demons nor men. Not that he fears death—no, he desires it. Why should he fear to live or fear to die when for him to live is Christ, and to die is gain? [13] Gladly and faithfully he stands for Christ, but he would prefer to be dissolved and to be with Christ, by far the beter thing.[14]

Go forth confidently then, you knights, and repel the foes of the cross of Christ[15] with a stalwart heart. Know that neither death nor life can separate you from the love of God which is in Jesus Christ,[16] and in every peril repeat, "Whether we live or whether we die, we are the Lord's."[17] What a glory to return in victory from such a battle! How blessed to die there as a martyr! Rejoice, brave athlete, if you live and conquer in the Lord; but glory and exult even more if you die and join your Lord. Life indeed is a fruitful thing and victory is glorious, but a holy death is more important than either. If they are blessed who die in the Lord,[18] how much more are they who die for the Lord!

2. To be sure, precious in the eyes of the Lord is the death of his holy ones,[19] whether they die in battle or in bed, but death in battle is more precious as it is the more glorious. How secure is life when the conscience is unsullied! How secure, I say, is life when death is anticipated without fear; or rather when it is desired with feeling and embraced with reverence! How holy and secure this knighthood and how

---

9. Ps 44:4. (The Vulgate - Douay ennumeration is followed for the Psalms as being the one with which Bernard was familiar.)

10. Lk 22:38. See Ep 256, PL 182:463-465; LBJ, Ep 399, pp. 470-472, and Csi 4:7, OB 3:454, for Bernard's doctrine on the two swords.

11. I.e., with the cross.

12. 1 Thess 5:8.	16. Rom 3:38.
13. Phil 1:21.	17. Rom 14:8.
14. Phil 1:23.	18. Rev 14:13.
15. Phil 3:18.	19. Ps 115:15.

entirely free of the double risk run by those men who fight not for Christ! Whenever you go forth, O worldly warrior, you must fear lest the bodily death of your foe should mean your own spiritual death, or lest perhaps your body and soul together should be slain by him.

Indeed, danger or victory for a Christian depends on the dispositions of his heart and not on the fortunes of war. If he fights for a good reason, the issue of his fight can never be evil; and likewise the results can never be considered good if the reason were evil and the intentions perverse. If you happen to be killed while you are seeking only to kill another, you die a murderer. If you succeed, and by your will to overcome and to conquer you perchance kill a man, you live a murderer. Now it will not do to be a murderer, living or dead, victorious or vanquished. What an unhappy victory—to have conquered a man while yielding to vice, and to indulge in an empty glory at his fall when wrath and pride have gotten the better of you!

But what of those who kill neither in the heat of revenge nor in the swelling of pride, but simply in order to save themselves? Even this sort of victory I would not call good, since bodily death is really a lesser evil than spiritual death. The soul need not die when the body does. No, it is the soul which sins that shall die.[20]

20. Ezek 18:4.

CHAPTER TWO

ON WORDLY KNIGHTHOOD

WHAT, THEN IS THE END OR FRUIT of this worldly knighthood, or rather knavery, as I should call it? What if not the mortal sin of the victor and the eternal death of the vanquished? Well then, let me borrow a word from the Apostle and exhort him who plows, to plow in hope, and him who threshes, to do so in view of some fruit.[1]

What then, O knights, is this monstrous error and what this unbearable urge which bids you fight with such pomp and labor, and all to no purpose except death and sin? You cover your horses with silk, and plume your armor with I know not what sort of rags; you paint your shields and your saddles; you adorn your bits and spurs with gold and silver and precious stones, and then in all this glory you rush to your ruin with fearful wrath and fearless folly. Are these the trappings of a warrior or are they not rather the trinkets of a woman? Do you think the swords of your foes will be turned back by your gold, spare your jewels or be unable to pierce your silks?

As you yourselves have often certainly experienced, a warrior especially needs these three things—he must guard his person with strength, shrewdness and care; he must be free in his movements, and he must be quick to draw his sword. Then why do you blind yourselves with effeminate locks and trip yourselves up with long and full tunics, burying your

1. 1 Cor 9:10.

tender, delicate hands in big cumbersome sleeves? Above all, there is that terrible insecurity of conscience, in spite of all your armor, since you have dared to undertake such a dangerous business on such slight and frivolous grounds. What else is the cause of wars and the root of disputes among you, except unreasonable flashes of anger, the thirst for empty glory,[2] or the hankering after some earthly possessions? It certainly is not safe to kill or to be killed for such causes as these.

2. Gal 5:26.

CHAPTER THREE

ON THE NEW KNIGHTHOOD

BUT THE KNIGHTS OF CHRIST may safely fight the battles of their Lord, fearing neither sin if they smite the enemy, nor danger at their own death; since to inflict death or to die for Christ is no sin, but rather, an abundant claim to glory. In the first case one gains for Christ, and in the second one gains Christ himself. The Lord freely accepts the death of the foe who has offended him, and yet more freely gives himself for the consolation of his fallen knight.

The knight of Christ,[1] I say, may strike with confidence and die yet more confidently, for he serves Christ when he strikes, and serves himself when he falls. Neither does he bear the sword in vain, for he is God's minister,[2] for the punishment of evildoers and for the praise of the good.[3] If he kills an evildoer, he is not a mankiller, but, if I may so put it, a killer of evil. He is evidently the avenger of Christ towards evildoers[4] and he is rightly considered a defender of Christians. Should he be killed himself, we know that he has not perished, but has come safely into port. When he inflicts death it is to Christs profit, and when he suffers death, it is for his own gain.[5] The Christian glories in the death of the pagan, because Christ is glorified; while the death of the Christian gives occasion for the King to show his liberality in

1. 2 Tim 2:3.
2. Rom 13:4.
3. 1 Pet 2:14.

4. Rom 13:4.
5. Phil 1:21.

the rewarding of his knight. In the one case the just shall rejoice when he sees justice done,[6] and in the other man shall say, truly there is a reward for the just; truly it is God who judges the earth.[7]

I do not mean to say that the pagans are to be slaughtered when there is any other way to prevent them from harassing and persecuting the faithful, but only that it now seems better to destroy them than that the rod of sinners be lifted over the lot of the just, and the righteous perhaps put forth their hands unto iniquity.[8]

5. What then? If it is never permissible for a Christian to strike with the sword, why did the Savior's precursor bid the soldiers to be content with their pay,[9] and not rather forbid them to follow this calling? But if it is permitted to all those so destined by God, as is indeed the case provided they have not embraced a higher calling, to whom, I ask, may it be allowed more rightly than to those whose hands and hearts hold for us Sion, the city of our strength? [10]

Thus when the transgressors of divine law have been expelled, the righteous nation that keeps the truth may enter in security.[11] Certainly it is proper that the nations who love war should be scattered,[12] that those who trouble us should be cut off,[13] and that all the workers of iniquity should be dispersed from the city of the Lord.[14] They busy themselves to carry away the incalculable riches placed in Jerusalem by the Christian peoples, to profane the holy things[15] and to possess the sanctuary of God as their heritage.[16] Let both swords[17] of the faithful fall upon the necks of the foe, in order to destroy every high thing exalting itself against the knowledge of God,[18] which is the Christian faith, lest the Gentiles should then say, "Where is their God? "[19]

6. Ps 57:11.
7. Ps 57:12.
8. Ps 124:3.
9. Lk 3:14.
10. Is 26:1.
11. Is 26:2.
12. Ps 67:31.

13. Gal 5:12.
14. Ps 100:8.
15. Lev 19:8.
16. Ps 82:13.
17. Lk 22:38. See above, c. 1, note 10.
18. 2 Cor 10:4-5.
19. Ps 113:2.

6. Once they have been cast out, he shall return to his heritage and to his house, which aroused his anger in the Gospel, "Behold," he said, "your house is left to you desolate."[20] He had complained through the Prophet: "I have left my house, I have forsaken my heritage,"[21] and he will fulfill that other prophecy: "The Lord has ransomed his people and delivered them.[22] They shall come and exult on Mount Sion, and rejoice in the good things of the Lord."[23]

Rejoice Jerusalem,[24] and recognize now the time in which you are visited! [25] Be glad and give praise together, wastes of Jerusalem, for the Lord has comforted his people. He has ransomed Jerusalem. The Lord has bared his holy arm in the sight of all peoples.[26] O virgin of Israel, you were fallen and there was none to raise you up.[27] Arise now and shake off the dust, O virgin, captive daughter of Sion.[28] Arise, I say, and stand on high. See the happiness which comes to you from your God.[29] You will no longer be referred to as the forsaken one, nor your land any more termed a wilderness; for the Lord takes his delight in you, and your land shall be peopled.[30] Raise your eyes, look about you and see; all these are gathered together and come to you.[31] Here is the help sent to you from the Holy One! [32] Through them is already fulfilled the ancient promise, "I will make you the pride of the ages, a joy from generation to generation. You will suck the milk of the nations and be nourished at the breasts of their sovereignty."[33] And again, "As a mother consoles her

20. Mt 23:38.
21. Jer 12:7.
22. Ps 76:16.
23. Jer 31:11-12. Bernard has fused this passage with the above text from Ps 76.
24. Roman missal, Introit for the 4th Sunday of Lent. Is 66:10.
25. Lk 19:44.
26. Is 52:9-10.
27. Amos 5:2.
28. Is 52:2.
29. Roman missal, Communion verse for 2nd Sunday of Advent. Bar 4:36; 5:5.
30. Is 62:4.
31. Is 49:18.
32. Ps 19:3.
33. Is 60:15-16.

children, so will I console you, and in Jerusalem you will be comforted."[34]

Do you not see how frequently these ancient witnesses foreshadowed the new knighthood? Truly, as we have heard, so we have now seen in the city of the Lord of armies.[35] Of course we must not let these literal fulfillments blind us to the spiritual meaning of the texts,[36] for we must live in eternal hope in spite of such temporal realizations of prophetic utterances. Otherwise the tangible would supplant the intangible, material poverty would threaten spiritual wealth[37] and present possessions would forestall future fulfillment. Furthermore, the temporal glory of the earthly city does not eclipse the glory of its heavenly counterpart, but rather prepares for it, at least so long as we remember that the one is the figure of the other, and that it is the heavenly one which is our mother.[38]

---

34. Is 66:13.
35. Ps 47:9.
36. Bernard, like all the Cistercian Fathers, in line with the whole patristic tradition, placed great emphasis on the spiritual interpretation of the Scriptures. See, e.g. SC 73:1-2: "Such is the literal sense, the portion of the Jews. But as for me, following the counsel of the Lord, I will search for the treasure of the spirit and life hidden in the profound depths of these inspired words."—OB 2:234. Many other examples could be given. For the fullest study of the various sense of Scripture and their use by the Fathers, see H. De Lubac, *Exégèse Médiéval,* 4 vols. (Paris: Aubier, 1959-1964).
37. The Cistercain ideal of poverty, which was taken over by the Knights, was a very real one, but a moderate one, with the emphasis on poverty of spirit and dependence on the Father of the Monastery, all things being held in common. See, e.g., Guerric of Igny: "What I have said is not new to you, my brethren, but I still want to impress upon you that truly blessed poverty of spirit is to be found more in humility of heart than in a mere privation of everyday possessions, and it consists more in the renunciation of pride than in a mere contempt for property. Sometimes it may be useful to own things. . . ." - OS, 53:5, CF 32:209.
38. Gal 4:26. Bernard saw some sacramental significance in the use of material things, but basically he was quite negative on their role in the spiritual life. See, e.g., Apo 28: "Bishops have a duty toward wise and foolish. They have to make use of material ornamentation to rouse devotion in a carnal people, incapable of spiritual things."—OB 3:104-105, CF 1:64.

CHAPTER FOUR

ON THE LIFE STYLE OF THE KNIGTS OF THE TEMPLE

AND NOW AS A MODEL, or at least for the shame of those knights of ours who are fighting for the devil rather than for God, we will briefly set forth the life and virtues of these cavaliers of Christ. Let us see how they conduct themselves at home as well as in battle, how they appear in public, and in what way the knight of God differs from the knight of the world.[1]

In the first place, discipline is in no way lacking and obedience is never despised. As Scripture testifies, the undisciplined son[2] shall perish and rebellion is as the sin of witchcraft, to refuse obedience is like the crime of idolatry.[3] Therefore they come and go at the bidding of their superior.[4] They wear what he gives them,[5] and do not presume to wear or to eat anything from another source.[6] Thus they shun every excess in clothing and food[7] and content themselves with what is necessary. They live as brothers in joyful and sober company, without wives or children. So that their evangelical perfection will lack nothing, they dwell united in one family[8]

---

1. The *Rule of the Knights Templars* should be seen in comparison with this chapter. Composed of 72 chapters like its model, Benedict's *Rule for Monasteries* (RB), the first draft was made by Bernard at the behest of the Council of Troyes (1128) which approved the Knights of the Temple. The revised Rule can be found in G. Schnürer, *Die Ursprüngliche Templerregel* (Freiburg-im-Breisgau, 1903), pp. 129-153; a summary is given by Ailbe Luddy, *The Life and Teaching of St Bernard* (Dublin: Gill, 1950), p. 173.

2. Sir 22:3.
3. 1 Sam 15:23.
4. Lk 7:8.
5. RB 55.

6. Cf. RB 51.
7. Cf. RB 29:7-9.
8. Ps 67:7.

with no personal property whatever,[9] careful to keep the unity of the Spirit in the bond of peace.[10] You may say that the whole multitude has but one heart and one soul[11] to the point that nobody follows his own will, but rather seeks to follow the commander.[12]

They never sit in idleness or wander about aimlessly,[13] but on the rare occasions when they are not on duty, they are always careful to earn their bread[14] by repairing their worn armor and torn clothing, or simply by setting things to order. For the rest, they are guided by the common needs and by the orders of their master.[15]

There is no distinction of persons among them,[16] and deference is shown to merit rather than to noble blood.[17] They rival one another in mutual consideration,[18] and they carry one another's burdens, thus fulfilling the law of Christ.[19] No inappropriate word, idle deed, unrestrained laugh, not even the slightest whisper or murmur is left uncorrected once it has been detected.[20] They foreswear dice and chess, and abhor the chase; they take no delight in the ridiculous cruelty of falconry, as is the custom. As for jesters, magicians, bards, troubadours and jousters, they despise and reject them as so many vanities and unsound deceptions.[21] Their hair is worn short, in conformity with the Apostle's saying, that it is shameful for a man to cultivate flowing locks.[22] Indeed, they seldom wash[23] and never set their hair—content to appear tousled and dusty, bearing the marks of the sun and of their armor.

8. When the battle is at hand, they arm themselves interiorly with faith and exteriorly with steel rather than decorate themselves with gold, since their business is to strike fear in the enemy rather than to incite his cupidity. They seek out

9. RB 55:16-18.
10. Eph 4:3.
11. Acts 4:32.
12. RB 4:60-61.
13. Cf. RB 48:1.
14. 2 Thes 3:8.
15. RB 48:3, 11.
16. Rom 2:11.

17. RB 2:20-22; 63:1, 7-8.
18. Rom 12:10; RB 72:4.
19. Gal 6:2.
20. RB 4:7.
21. Ps 39:5.
22. 1Cor 11:14.
23. RB 36:8.

horses which are strong and swift, rather than those which are brilliant and well-plumed, they set their minds on fighting to win rather than on parading for show. They think not of glory and seek to be formidable rather than flamboyant. At the same time, they are not quarrelsome, rash, or unduly hasty, but soberly, prudently and providently drawn up into orderly ranks, as we read of the fathers.[24] Indeed, the true Israelite[25] is a man of peace,[26] even when he goes forth to battle.

Once he finds himself in the thick of battle, this knight sets aside his previous gentleness, as if to say, "Do I not hate those who hate you, O Lord; am I not disgusted with your enemies? "[27] These men at once fall violently upon the foe, regarding them as so many sheep. No matter how outnumbered they are, they never regard these as fierce barbarians or as awe-inspiring hordes. Nor do they presume on their own strength,[28] but trust in the Lord of armies to grant them the victory.[29] They are mindful of the words of Maccabees, "It is simple enough for a multitude to be vanquished by a handful. It makes no difference to the God of heaven whether he grants deliverance by the hands of few or many; for victory in war is not dependent on a big army, and bravery is the gift of heaven."[30] On numerous occasions they had seen one man pursue a thousand, and two put ten thousand to flight.[31]

Thus in a wonderous and unique manner they appear gentler than lambs, yet fiercer than lions. I do not know if it would be more appropriate to refer to them as monks or as soldiers, unless perhaps it would be better to recognize them as being both. Indeed they lack neither monastic meekness nor military might. What can we say of this, except that this

24. 2 Mac 12:20; see also 8:23 and 1 Mac 4:41.
25. Jn 1:47.
26. Gen 42:31; Mt 5:9.
27. Ps 138:21.
28. Judg 7:2.
29. 2 Mac 15:8; Jer 11:20.
30. 1 Mac 3:18-10.
31. Deut 32:30; 2 Mac 8:19-20.

CF 19: Bernard of Clairvaux: Treatises III

ERRATA ET CORRIGENDA

Pg. 117, note 7: read c. 3, pp. 132-3 for c. 3, p.00.
Pg. 118, note 11: read c. 7, pp. 148-9 for p. 00.
Pg. 119, notes 13 & 16: read p. 135 for p. 00.
Pg. 122, note 23: read p. 156 for p. 00.
        note 24: read p. 157 for p. 00.
        note 25: read pp. 154-65 for pp. 00-00.
Pg. 126, note 5: read p. 137 for p. 00.
Pg. 138, note 1, line 3: read Bernard may have collaborated in drawing
        up the first draft for The first draft was made by Bernard....
        note 1: insert in line 5: PL 166:853-73 and in G. Schnürer....
Pg. 140, note 30: read 3:18 & 19 for 3:18-10.
Pg. 155, line 8: read law of talion for law of talon.
Pg. 166, para. 3, line 1: read Pressed as I am for Dressed as I am....
Pg. 171, line 7: read croisade for crusade.
        line 10: read Règle des Templiers for Règle du Templiers.

has been done by the Lord, and it is marvelous in our eyes.[32] These are the picked troops of God, whom he has recruited from the ends of the earth; the valiant men of Israel chosen to guard well and faithfully that tomb which is the bed of the true Solomon, each man sword in hand, and superbly trained to war.[33]

32. Ps 117:23.
33. Song 3:7-8.

CHAPTER FIVE

THE TEMPLE OF JERUSALEM

THEIR QUARTERS indeed are in the very temple of Jerusalem, which is not as vast as the ancient masterpiece of Solomon, but is no less glorious. Truly all the magnificence of the first temple lay in perishable gold and silver,[1] in polished stones and precious woods;[2] whereas all the beauty and gracious charming adornment of its present counterpart is the religious fervor of its occupants and by their well-disciplined behavior. In the former, one could contemplate all sorts of beautiful colors, while in the latter one is able to venerate all sorts of virtues and good works. Indeed holiness is the fitting ornament for God's house.[3] One is able to delight there in splendid merits rather than in shining marble, and to be captivated by pure hearts rather than by gilded paneling.

Of course the facade of this temple is adorned, but with weapons rather than with jewels, and in place of the ancient golden crowns, its walls are hung round about with shields.[4] In place of candlesticks, censers and ewers, this house is well furnished with saddles, bits and lances. By all these signs our knights clearly show that they are animated by the same zeal for the house of God which of old passionately inflamed their leader himself when he armed his most holy hands, not indeed with a sword, but with a whip. Having fashioned this

1. 1 Pet 1:18.
2. 1 Kings 6ff.
3. Ps 92:5.
4. 1 Mac 4:57.

from some lengths of cord, he entered the temple and ejected the merchants, scattered the coins of the money changers, and overturned the chairs of the pigeon venders, considering it most unfitting to defile this house of prayer by such traffic.[5]

Moved therefore by their King's example, his devoted soldiers consider that it is even more shameful and infinitely more intolerable for a holy place to be polluted by pagans[6] than to be crowded with merchants. Once they have installed themselves in this holy house with their horses and their weapons, cleansed it and the other holy places of every un-Christian stain, and cast out the tyrannical horde, they occupy themselves day and night in both pious exercises and practical work. They are especially careful to honor the temple of God with zealous and sincere reverence, offering by their devout service, not the flesh of animals according to the ancient rites,[7] but true peace offerings of brotherly love, devoted obedience and voluntary poverty.

10. These events at Jerusalem have shaken the world. The islands hearken, and the people from afar give ear.[8] They swarm forth from East and West, as a flood stream bringing glory to the nations[9] and a rushing river gladdening the city of God.[10] What could be more profitable and pleasant to behold than seeing such a multitude coming to reinforce the few? What, if not the twofold joy of seeing the conversion of these former impious rogues, sacrilegious thieves, murderers, perjurers and adulterers?[11] A twofold joy and a twofold benefit, since their countrymen are as glad to be rid of them as their new comrades are to receive them. Both sides have profited from this exchange, since the latter are strengthened and the former are now left in peace. Thus Egypt rejoices in

---

5. Mt 21:12-13, Jn 2:14-16. This Gospel scene was probably enacted on the very site of the Templar's quarters, the royal porch of Herod's temple and the present mosque El Aksa.

6. Lev 19:8.

7. 1 Kings 8:63.

8. Is 49:1.

9. Is 66:12.

10. Ps 45:5.

11. 1 Tim 1:9-10.

their conversion and departure[12] while Mount Sion rejoices and the daughters of Juda are glad[13] to acquire these new protectors. The former glory in being delivered from their hands,[14] while the latter have every reason to expect deliverance by means of these same hands. The former gladly see their cruel despoilers depart, while the latter gladly welcome their faithful defenders; so that the one is agreeably heartened, while the other is profitably abandoned.

This is the revenge which Christ contrives against his enemies,[15] to triumph powerfully and gloriously over them by their own means. Indeed, it is both a happy and fitting thing that those who have so long fought against him should at last fight for him. Thus he recruits his soldiers among his foes, just as he once turned Saul the persecutor into Paul the preacher.[16] Therefore I am not surprised that, as our Savior himself has affirmed, the court of heaven takes more joy in the conversion of one sinner than in the virtues of many just men who have no need of conversion.[17] Certainly the conversion of so many sinners and evil doers will now do as much good as their former misdeeds did harm.

11. Hail then, holy city,[18] sanctified by the Most High for his own tabernacle[19] in order that such a generation might be saved in and through you! Hail, city of the great King,[20] source of so many joyous and unheard-of marvels! Hail mistress of nations and queen of provinces,[21] heritage of patriarchs,[22] mother of apostles and prophets, source of the faith and glory of the Christian people! If God has permitted you to be so often beseiged, it has only been to furnish brave men an occasion for valor and immortality.

Hail promised land, source of milk and honey for your ancient inhabitants,[23] now become the source of healing

---

12. Ps 104:38; Ex 12:33, 36. The Latin *profectus* here has a double meaning: conversion and departure.

13. Ps 47:12.
14. Lk 1:74.
15. Nahum 1:2.
16. Acts 9:1-22.
17. Lk 15:7.
18. Is 52:1.

19. Ps 45:5.
20. Ps 47:3.
21. Lam 1:1.
22. Gen 17:8.
23. Ex 3:8.

grace and vital sustenance for the whole earth! Yes, I say, you are that good and excellent soil which received into its fruitful depths the heavenly seed from the heart of the eternal Father.[24] What a rich harvest of martyrs you have produced from that heavenly seed! Your fertile soil has not failed to furnish splendid examples of every Christian virtue for the whole earth—some bearing fruit thirtyfold, some sixty, and some a hundredfold.[25] Therefore those who have seen you are most happily filled with the great abundance of your sweetness and are well nourished on your munificent bounty.[26] Everywhere they go they publish the fame of your great goodness[27] and relate the splendors of your glory[28] to those who have never seen it, proclaiming the marvels[29] accomplished in you even to the ends of the earth.[30]

Indeed, glorious things are told of you, city of God! [31] Now then we will set forth something of the delights in which you abound, for the praise and glory of your name.

24. Lk 8:15.
25. Mt 13:23.
26. Ps 30:20.
27. Ps 144:7.
28. Ps 144-5.
29. Sir 36:10.
30. Is 49:6. See also, Acts 1:8, 13:47.
31. Ps 86:3.

CHAPTER SIX

BETHLEHEM

BEFORE ALL ELSE, for the nourishment of holy souls[1] you have Bethlehem, the house of bread. It was there that he first appeared—he, the living bread come down from heaven,[2] born of the Virgin. There the docile draft animal may yet find the crib,[3] and in the crib the straw from the virgin field; and there the ox may recognize his owner, and the ass the manger of his Lord.[4] Indeed, all flesh is as grass, and all its glory is as the wildflower.[5] Since man failed to recognize the honor in which he was made, he has been likened to the dumb beasts, and is made like them.[6] That is why the Word of God and the Bread of Angels has become the food of animals—so that in ruminating on this fodder man might regain his lost dignity. He had all but lost his taste for the bread of the word, but now it is restored to him by the Word made flesh.

No longer a beast, but a man again, he may say with St Paul, "If we have known Christ according to the flesh, we know him so no longer."[7] This I feel nobody can truly say unless he has with Peter first heard from the mouth of Truth this other saying, "The words which I have spoken to you are spirit and life, but the flesh is of no profit."[8] He who has found life in the words of Christ no longer seeks the flesh.[9]

1. Wis 3:13.
2. Jn 6:51.
3. Lk 2:7.
4. Is 1:3.
5. Is 40:6.

6. Ps 48:13.
7. 2 Cor 5:16.
8. Jn 6:64.
9. Prov 8:35.

He is now one of those blessed ones who believe without seeing.[10] Only a child needs milk,[11] and only an animal feeds on hay.[12] But he who does not offend in word is a perfect man,[13] worthy of solid food.[14] Even if he has to sweat for it,[15] he is able to eat the bread of the word without offense. He will not be afraid to speak the wisdom of God when he is in the company of perfect men,[16] comparing one spiritual truth with another.[17] There will be no scandal. However when he is with children or the beasts of the herd, he will be careful to adjust himself to their capacity, and to speak only of Christ and of his cross.[18]

Nevertheless it is one and the same sweet nourishment from the heavenly pastures which furnishes fodder for animals and bread for men, a source of strength for adults and of growth for the immature.

10. Jn 20:29.
11. 1 Cor 3:2.
12. Ps 103:14.
13. Jas 3:2.
14. Heb 5:14.

15. Gen 3:19.
16. 1 Cor 2:6.
17. 1 Cor 2:13.
18. 1 Cor 2:2.

CHAPTER SEVEN

NAZARETH

T HERE, TOO, ONE MAY SEE NAZARETH—that is to say, the flower. It was here that the infant God born in Bethlehem grew to maturity, as the fruit matures within the flower. Just as a perfume of the flower precedes the savor of the fruit, so the nostrils of the prophets preceded the lips of the apostles, each in turn pervaded by this holy savor. The Jew had to content himself with an ephemeral perfume, while the Christian may nourish himself on the solid food. Indeed, Nathanael had perceived this flower whose scent was sweeter than any ointment,[1] and that is why he asked, "Can anything good come from Nazareth? "[2] He was not content with the odor alone, for he accepted Philip's invitation to come and see.[3] Indeed, he was already captivated by the wondrous sweetness of his scent, and all the more eager to taste the fruit as he inhaled its fragrance. Led on by the odor he hastened without delay to the fruit. He wanted to confirm in the concrete what he had as yet only vaguely sensed, and taste what he had savored from afar.

Let us see if we can not perhaps shed some light on this passage by comparing it to the perception of the Patriarch Isaac. Scripture says of him that, "As soon as he had perceived the fragrance of his son's garments (Jacob's, of course) he said, 'Behold, the odor of my son is as the odor of a fruitful field which the Lord has blessed.' "[4] He perceived

1. Song 4:10.
2. Jn 1:46.
3. Ibid.
4. Gen 27:27.

148

the fragrance of the garments, but he did not recognize the person whom they covered. He was captivated by the mere odor of these garments in an exterior manner, as by the fragrance of a flower, without being able to taste the savor of the hidden fruit; since he was as yet ignorant of the sacred destiny for which this son of his had been chosen.[5]

What is the meaning of all this? The garment is the spirit of the Word, and the letter is his flesh, but now the Jews are not able to recognize either the Word in flesh, the divinity in man, or the spiritual sense hidden beneath the written word. They feel only the goat skin covering which resembles the elder brother,[6] that is, the sinful Adam, and they are not able to attain the naked truth. He did not assume sinful flesh, but only "the likeness of sinful flesh,"[7] since he had come to take away sin[8] and not to commit it.[9]

He appeared thus as he himself proclaimed, so that the blind might see, and the clear sighted might become blind.[10] Just as the Prophet was then deceived by appearances,[11] so the blind of our day bless him whom they know not.[12] They read of him in their books,[13] but fail to recognize him in his mighty deeds. They have touched him with their own hands,[14] bound him,[15] scourged him[16] and buffeted him,[17] but without realizing that he was to rise from the dead.[18] If they had known, they would never have crucified the Lord of glory.[19]

We will say a few words about the other holy places, though our incapacity will oblige us to leave much unsaid. At least we may speak of some of their more striking aspects, albeit briefly.

---

5. Gen 25:23.
6. Gen 27:22-23.
7. Rom 8:3.
8. Jn 1:29.
9. 1 Pet 2:22.
10. Jn 9:39.
11. Gen 27:27.
12. Jn 4:22.

13. 2 Cor 3:15.
14. Gen 27:12.
15. Jn 18:12.
16. Jn 19:1.
17. Mt 26:67.
18. Jn 2:20-21.
19. 1 Cor 2:8.

CHAPTER EIGHT

THE MOUNT OF OLIVES AND THE VALLEY OF JOSAPHAT

IN ORDER TO CLIMB the Mount of Olives one must descend into the valley of Josaphat, so that in contemplating the richness of divine mercy one may not forget the fear of judgment. If in the abundance of his mercy he is always inclined to forgive,[1] his judgments are nonetheless exceedingly deep[2] and are recognized as extremely terrifying for the sons of men.[3] David shows us the Mount of Olives saying, "You rescue both man and beast, O Lord; in the generous outpouring of your mercy."[4] God refers to the valley of judgment in the same Psalm: "Let not the steps of pride approach me, nor let the hands of sinners shake me."[5] Evidently he is afraid of sharing their lot, as is plain from another Psalm where he prays, "Pierce my flesh with your fear; indeed I am afraid of your judgments."[6]

This is the valley into which the proud fall and are crushed, while the humble descend in all security. The proud man excuses his sin, but the humble man accuses himself, knowing that God will not judge him a second time,[7] and that if we judge ourselves we shall indeed escape judgment.[8]

15. Furthermore, the proud man does not consider how terrible it is to fall into the hands of the living God,[9] so that he easily excuses his sins with evil words.[10] It is a great per-

1. Is 55:7.
2. Ps 35:7.
3. Ps 65:5.
4. Ps 35:7-8.
5. Ps 35:12.
6. Ps 118:120.
7. Nahum 1:9 (Septuagint).
8. 1 Cor 11:31.
9. Heb 10:31.
10. Ps 140:4.

versity not to have mercy on yourself, and to reject the only remedy of confessing your sins. Instead of shaking off the burning coals, you clasp them to your bosom,[11] and refuse to heed the advice of the Wise Man who said, "Please God by having mercy on your own soul."[12] Likewise, if a man does evil to himself, to whom will he do good? [13] "Now the world is being judged, now the prince of this world is cast forth."[14] You can cast him forth from your heart if you judge yourself in humility. The judgment of heaven will take place when heaven itself will be judged from above, and the earth, too, that God might single out his people.[15] You should fear lest you, too, should then be cast out with the prince and his angels,[16] if you should be found to be one who has not already been judged.

Indeed, the spiritual man who judges all things is himself judged by no man.[17] That is why judgment begins with the house of God,[18] so that at his coming the Judge will find that his own followers, whom he recognizes,[19] have already been judged. And then he will have no further judgment to pronounce on them, when he shall come rather to judge those who labor not as common men and suffer not from the common scourges.[20]

11. Prov 6:27.
12. Sir 30:24.
13. Sir 14:5.
14. Jn 12:31.
15. Ps 49:4.

16. Mt 25:41.
17. 1 Cor 2:15.
18. 1 Pet 4:17.
19. Jn 10:14; 13:18.
20. Ps 72:5.

CHAPTER NINE

THE JORDAN

HOW JOYFULLY does the Jordan clasp Christians to its bosom—that river which glories in being sanctified by the baptism of Christ! Certainly that Syrian leper was mistaken who preferred I know not what waters of Damascus to those of Israel,[1] to the waters of our river Jordan, which have ever shown themselves so docile to God! Marvelously they parted to leave a dry path for both Elijah and Elisha,[2] and also in an earlier age when they held back their force for Josue and for all the people.[3] Furthermore, what river can claim pre-eminence over this one which the Trinity has dedicated to itself by a manifest presence? The Father was heard, the Holy Spirit was seen, and the Son was baptized.[4] It is no wonder then that just as those waters restored health to the limbs of Naaman at the bidding of the Prophet, so the whole Christian people experiences their spiritual power at the command of Christ.[5]

1. 2 Kings 5:12.
2. 2 Kings 2:8, 14.
3. Josh 3:15; 4:18.

4. Lk 3:22.
5. 2 Kings 5:14.

CHAPTER TEN

MOUNT CALVARY

WE GO OUT INDEED TO MOUNT CALVARY[1] where as the true Elisha[2] was mocked by foolish servants[3] in order to win eternal joy for his sons, of whom he says, "Behold, I and my children whom God has given me."[4] These are good children who, unlike those evil ones,[5] heed the exhortation of the Psalmist, "Give praise, you children of the Lord; praise the name of the Lord."[6] Praise is perfected in the mouths of holy infants and sucklings[7] just as it is wanting in the mouths of the envious, of whom he complains, "I have raised my children and set them up, but they have spurned me."[8] Therefore our bared head went up himself,[9] ascending his cross. He is exposed to the world for the sake of the world, with uncovered head and unveiled face,[10] making atonement for sin.[11] He did not draw back from the disgrace of a cruel and shameful death in order to expiate our sins; nor did he shrink from its tortures in order to deliver us from eternal shame[12] and to restore us to glory. This should cause no surprise. What did he have to be ashamed of? He cleansed us from our sins,[13] not as water which itself becomes polluted as it washes, but as a sunbeam which dries up filth and itself remains pure. Indeed he is the very wisdom of God[14] whose purity penetrates everywhere.[15]

1. *Calvariae locum.* Jn 19:17.
2. 2 Kings 2:23.
3. Mt 27:39; Mk 14:65. Bernard is playing on the double meaning of the Latin *puer* which can mean either boy or servant.
4. Is 8:18; Heb 2:13.
5. 2 Kings 2:23; Ps 21:17.
6. Ps 112:1.
7. Ps 8:3.
8. Is 1:2.
9. 2 Kings 2:23.
10. 2 Cor 3:18.
11. Heb 1:3.
12. Ps 77:66; Jer 23:40.
13. Rev 1:5.
14. 1 Cor 1:24.
15. Wis 7:24.

CHAPTER ELEVEN

THE HOLY SEPULCHER

SOMEHOW THE HOLY SEPULCHER seems to be the most attractive of holy places. I do not know exactly why the devout are more drawn to the place where his dead body rested than to where he lived and worked,[1] or why the remembrance of his death should move us more than that of his life. Perhaps it is because the latter is regarded as more demanding, while the former is more satisfying; or that human weakness is more drawn by his peaceful repose than by strenuous activity, by the security of his death than by the rectitude of his life. The life of Christ has furnished me with a pattern for living, but his death has delivered me from death. The one prepared life, while the other destroyed death.[2] His life is as hard as his death is precious, but both are necessary. Is the death of Christ any more profit to a man whose life is evil than the life of Christ is to one who makes a bad end? Is the death of Christ any more able to deliver from eternal death those who now sin unto death than he was able by his life to liberate the saints who had died before his coming? Is it not written, "What living man will never see death, or is able to deliver his soul from the grip of Hell? "[3]

Now then, since it was necessary for us to live in holiness[4] and to die in confidence, he taught us how to live by his life and how to die by his death. Indeed he died as one destined to rise again, in order that men might die in the hope of rising again. But he has added a third gift, without which the other two would be of no profit, and that is the remission of sins. For what help toward his true and supreme happiness would

1. Bar 3:38.   3. Ps 88:49.
2. 2 Tim 1:10.   4. Tit 2:2.

154

a good or even an endless life be to one who was still bound, even if only by original sin? Death indeed is but the consequence of sin,[5] and if man had avoided sin he would never have tasted death.[6]

19. It was by sin then that man lost life and found death, for God had forewarned, and it was perfectly just, that if man sinned he would die.[7] What could be more just than the law of talon?[8] God is indeed the life of the soul, just as it is the life of the body. By willful sin it has willingly given up life, though it is unwilling to give up the body. It has freely rejected life since it did not wish to live; therefore it is no longer able to give life where and when it pleases. It did not want to be governed by God, therefore it is unable to govern its body. How can it command an inferior when it ignores its own superior? If the Creator has found his creature in revolt, the soul will find its footman a rebel as well. Man has been guilty of transgressing divine law,[9] so he finds another law in his members resisting the rule of reason and imprisoning him in the law of sin.[10]

Indeed it is written that sin separates us from God,[11] therefore death will separate us from our bodies as well. The soul cannot be separated from God except by sin, nor can the body be separated from the soul except by death. Where is the injustice of its punishment when it is only suffering from its subject the same revolt which it had contrived against its Creator? Nothing could be more fitting than that death should cause death—spiritual death causing a corporeal one, a culpable death causing one that is penal, and willful death one that is constrained.

Man was then condemned to a twofold death according to his double nature, a voluntary spiritual death and imposed physical death. The God-man mercifully and powerfully provided a remedy for both by his death, which was at the same time both physical and voluntary; and this one death of his

5. Rom 6:23.
6. Jn 8:51-52.
7. Gen 2:17.
8. Ex 21:23; Deut 19:21: "Life for life."

9. Jas 2:11.
10. Rom 7:23.
11. Is 59:2.

canceled our double death. This was indeed fitting, for the first of our two deaths was merited by our fault and the second indebted for our punishment. He took the punishment on himself without participating in the fault, and underwent a voluntary but only physical death in order to win for us both life and innocence. For if he had not suffered physically, he would not have paid the debt, and if he had not died willingly his death would have been without merit. Now then if the cause of death is sin and the consequence of sin is death, as we have seen, Christ in forgiving the sin and dying for sinners has both removed the cause and canceled the consequence.

21. But how do we know that Christ is able to forgive sins? No doubt it is because he is God[12] and can do whatever he wishes. But how do we know that he is God? It is proved by his miracles. He did things which nobody else was able to do,[13] not to mention the predictions of the Prophets[14] and the voice of the Father coming down to him from the majestic glory of heaven.[15] If God be with us, who is against us? [16] It is God who justifies, who can condemn? [17] If it is he and none other[18] to whom we daily confess, "Against you alone have I sinned,"[19] who better, or rather who else, can forgive what has been done against him alone? How could he not be able, who is able to do all things? [20] If I can forgive an offense against me at will, cannot God, too, remit offenses committed against him? If then the Almighty and he alone against whom we have sinned can forgive sins,[21] that man is indeed blessed to whom the Lord does not impute sin.[22] Therefore we know that Christ can remit sin by the power of his divinity.

22. And who can doubt that he is ready to do so? How could he refuse us his justice who has assumed our flesh and

---

12. Lk 5:21.
13. Jn 15:24.
14. Is 9:5.
15. 2 Pet 1:17; Mt 17:5.
16. Rom 8:31.
17. Rom 8:33-34.
18. Deut 4:35; Is 45:18.
19. Ps 50:6.
20. Wis 7:27; Mt 28:18.
21. Lk 5:21.
22. Ps 31:2.

even endured our death? He freely took flesh,[23] freely suffered and was freely crucified;[24] why then should he withhold only the gift of justification? Just as he is plainly able in virtue of his divinity, so he is evidently willing in virtue of his humanity.

But again, how do we know that he has really overcome death? Precisely in that he, who did not deserve it, underwent it. How could we be expected to pay a debt which he has already satisfied in our stead? He who has assumed the guilt of our sins while bestowing his justice upon us has himself paid our debt of death and restored us to life. Life will return once death is dead,[25] just as justice is reestablished when sin is removed. Indeed the death of Christ has put death to flight[26] and the justice of Christ is now counted as ours.

How could he have really died, he who was God? How, except that he was also man. But how could the death of one man be credited to another? How, except that this man was just.[27] Obviously he was able to die as a man; and as a just man it was fitting that he die to some purpose. Of course the death of one sinner does not suffice to pay the debt of another sinner, since each must die for himself. But why should the death of one who had no need to die for himself not be of profit to others? The more unjust the death of the innocent, the more justly will he for whom he dies live.

23. "But what kind of justice is this," you may say, "that the innocent should die for the guilty?"[28] It is not justice, but mercy. If it were justice, he would not have died freely, but under constraint. Thus if he had himself merited death he would have died indeed, but without winning life for others. But if this is not justice, neither is it contrary to justice. Otherwise he could not at the same time be both just and merciful.[29]

"If it be not unjust that a just man should be able to satisfy

23. Heb 10:7.
24. Jn 10:18.
25. Hos 13:14.
26. 1 Cor 15:54.

27. Lk 23:47.
28. 1 Pet 3:18; Rom 5:6.
29. 2 Mac 1:24.

for a sinner, yet how can one man satisfy the debts of many? It would seem that justice is stretched quite enough if one life is redeemed by another's death." The Apostle has already answered this; "Just as all men were condemned by the fault of one man," he says, "so all men receive the justification of life through the justice of one. Just as by the disobedience of one man many were made sinners, so by the obedience of one many will be made just."[30] But perhaps one who can restore justice to many cannot likewise restore life? "Death came by one man," he says, "and by one man life. Just as all died in Adam, so shall all receive life in Christ."[31] What would you have? One sins and all are held guilty; shall the innocence of the other profit him alone? The sin of one has caused the death of all; shall the justice of the other restore but one life? Is the justice of God then more apt to condemn than to pardon, or is Adam more efficacious in evil than Christ is in good? Shall the sin of Adam be counted against me, and the justice of Christ be unable to reach me? Shall the disobedience of the one damn me, and the obedience of the other not profit me?

24. "But," you will say, "we have all deserved to share in the guilt of Adam, since we have all participated in his sin.[32] When he sinned we were in him, and were begotten from his flesh according to the desire of the flesh."[33] Yes, but we are even more closely related to God by our birth according to the Spirit than to Adam by the flesh, since we were spiritually present in Christ long before our existence in the flesh of Adam. At least we were, if we may presume that we are counted among those of whom the Apostle said, "Who has chosen us in him (the Father, that is, in the Son) before the foundation of the world."[34] They are also born of God, according to the word of the evangelist John where he says, "who are born not of blood, nor of the will of the flesh, nor of the will of man, but of God."[35] Again in his letter he says,

---

30. Rom 5:18-19.
31. 1 Cor 15:21-22.
32. Rom 5:12.

33. 1 Jn 2:16.
34. Eph 1:4.
35. Jn 1:13.

"Whoever is born of God sins not,"[36] since his celestial origin preserves him.

"But," you say, "the presence of the carnal heritage is betrayed by carnal concupiscence, and the sin which we experience in the flesh clearly proves that we are the carnal posterity of the sinner's flesh." Yes, but the spiritual heritage is nonetheless experienced; not of course in the flesh, but in the hearts of those at least who can say with Paul, "We, however, have the mind of Christ."[37] These sense themselves to have progressed to the extent that they, themselves, can say in all confidence:[38] "The Spirit himself bears witness to our spirit that we are the sons of God;"[39] and again: "We have not received the spirit of this world, but the Spirit which is of God, in order that we might recognize the gifts we have received from God."[40] Therefore it is by the Spirit of God that his love is poured forth into our hearts,[41] just as it is by the flesh of Adam that concupiscence remains in our bodies. As the latter which derives from the flesh of the first father is never absent from bodies in this mortal life, so the former which originates from the Father of souls never departs[42] from the wills of his sons as long as they are true sons.

25. If we are then born of God[43] and chosen in Christ, why should justice require that our human and earthly origin should be more powerful in evil than our heavenly origin in good? Why should our fleshly heritage outweigh God's choice, and his eternal designs be frustrated by a carnal concupiscence which is merely temporal? If death came by one man,[44] why should not life all the more readily come from one who is perfect man? If we have all died in Adam, why should we not be much more powerfully vivified in Christ? [45] Indeed, "There is no proportion between the gift and the fault.[46] One fault brought on the sentence of condemnation,

36. 1 Jn 3:9.
37. 1 Cor 2:16.
38. Acts 4:29.
39. Rom 8:16.
40. 1 Cor 2:12.
41. Rom 5:5.

42. 1 Cor 13:8.
43. Jn 1:13.
44. Rom 5:12, 17.
45. 1 Cor 15:22.
46. Rom 5:15.

whereas many faults have now won the grace of justification."[47]

Therefore Christ could both forgive sins as God and die as man. In dying the death[48] he was able to pay our debt to death, because he was truly just.[49] The justice of one suffices to buy life and justice for all, seeing as the sin and death of one was communicated to all.

26. But it was also foreseen to be most necessary that he delay his death and live for a time as man among men, so that his daily words teaching men the truth might stimulate them to desire things invisible, that his mighty works might strengthen their faith and that his example might guide their conduct. Therefore the God-man lived a sober, pious and just life in the eyes of men;[50] he spoke the truth, worked wonders and suffered indignities. What was then lacking for our salvation, except that he add the grace of forgiveness of sins? Indeed he forgave sins gratuitously, and the work of our salvation was then complete.

It is not to be feared that as God, he lacked the power to remit sin; or that he lacked the will to do so as one who had suffered, and suffered so much, for sinners. This will be so, at least, if we are careful to imitate his example as we should, and likewise to venerate his miracles, to believe his teachings and to be grateful for his sufferings.

27. Everything therefore in Christ was for our profit, everything was necessary and salutary, his weakness no less than his majesty. If he removed the yoke of sin at a word by the power of his divinity, yet by the weakness of his flesh in dying he cancelled the rights of death. The Apostle expressed this beautifully when he said: "The weakness of God is stronger than men."[51] Yes, and even his foolishness by which it pleased him to save the world.[52] In order to refute worldly wisdom he confounds the wise,[53] since when he was in the form of God and equal to God he emptied himself, taking the form of a servant.[54] Rich as he was, he became poor for our

47. Rom 5:16.
48. Gen 2:17.
49. Lk 23:47.
50. Tit 2:12.

51. 1 Cor 1:25.
52. 1 Cor 1:21.
53. 1 Cor 1:27.
54. Phil 2:6-7.

sakes.[55] Great as he was, he became a little one,[56] and elevated as he was, humble.[57] He who was strong became weak, since he suffered hunger[58] and thirst,[59] since he became tired in his travels,[60] and suffered many other things from choice rather than from necessity. These were for him a sort of foolishness, but were they not for us the path of prudence,[61] the model of rectitude and the pattern of holiness? Therefore the Apostle also said: "The foolishness of God is wiser than men."[62]

His death then delivered us from death, his life from error, and his grace from sin. Indeed his death was victorious because of his justice, since in repaying what he had not stolen[63] the just one acquired a perfect right to reclaim what he had lost. As for his life, it constituted for us by its wisdom a model and mirror of life and knowledge,[64] and his grace indeed, as has been said, forgave sin by that very power which is able to do whatever it wills.[65] Therefore the death of Christ is the death of my death,[66] since he died that I might live. How could that man fail to be alive for whom Life had died? Likewise, who can still fear to go astray in the knowledge of life and reality when Wisdom is his guide? Again, how can he be held guilty whom Justice has absolved? He showed himself to us as Life in the Gospel when he said, "I am the Life."[67] As for the two others, we have the testimony of the Apostle who said: "He is become for us Justice and Wisdom unto God the Father."[68]

28. If then the law of the Spirit of Life has delivered us in Jesus Christ from the law of sin and death,[69] why do we still have to die, instead of being at once clothed with immortality?[70] Truly, that the truth of God might be accom-

60. Jn 4:6.
61. Is 40:14.
62. 1 Cor 1:25.
63. Ps 68:5.
64. Sir 45:6.
65. Ps 134:6. See above, no. 21.
66. Hos 13:14.
67. Jn 14:6.
68. 1 Cor 1:30. Paul did not say "the Father" but implies it.
69. Rom 8:2.
70. 1 Cor 15:53; 2 Cor 5:3.

55. 2 Cor 8:9.
56. Is 9:6.
57. Mt 11:29.
58. Mt 4:2.
59. Jn 19:28.

plished, for God has loved both mercy and truth.[71] Therefore it is necessary that man die, as God has foretold;[72] but also that he rise from dead,[73] lest God should forget his mercy.[74] Although death is not to reign forever, it still remains with us now because of God's truth.[75] In the same way sin is not quite absent from us, though it no longer reigns in our mortal bodies.[76] Furthermore Paul glories in his partial liberation from the law of sin and death,[77] yet he still complains that he is encumbered by both these forces in a certain measure. He cries out against the law of sin, protesting, "I find another law in my members . . ."[78] and he also groans beneath the burden (doubtless of the law of death) awaiting the redemption of his body."[79]

29. These thoughts and similar ones regarding the holy sepulcher present themselves to the reflection of Christians according to the attractions of each.[80] Still I think that those who are actually able to see even with their bodily eyes and the bodily resting place of the Lord must experience the strongest emotions, from which they will receive no little profit. Even though this place is now empty of its sacred contents, it remains full of delightful mysteries for us—for us, I say, because it is really our resting place. At least it is if we take seriously what we certainly remember the Apostle to have said: "By baptism we are buried together with Christ in death, so that just as Christ rose from the dead for the glory of his Father, so we too may walk in newness of life. If we have been buried together with him in the likeness of his death, so shall we be raised up with him."[81]

How sweet it must be for pilgrims after the fatigue of their long journey and their many perils on land and sea[82] to find rest there at last—there where they know their own Lord has rested! I should think that in their joy they no longer feel

---

71. Ps 83:12; Ps 84:11.
72. Gen 2:17, 3:19.
73. Is 26:19; Mt 16:21.
74. Ps 76:10.
75. Rom 15:8.
76. Rom 6:12.
77. Rom 8:2.
78. Rom 7:23.
79. 2 Cor 5:4.
80. Rom 14:5. The Greek has "opinions" instead of "attractions."
81. Rom 6:4-5.
82. 2 Cor 11:26.

their weariness, nor regret their expenses, but claim the reward of their labor and the prize of their course[83] according to the words: "They rejoice exceedingly to have found the tomb."[84]

We need not be so foolish as to suppose that the holy sepulcher gained this fame by accident or by the fickle winds of popular favor, but rather we should recognize that Isaiah foretold this ages ago: "In that day the root of Jesse will stand as a banner before the peoples, the gentiles shall entreat him and his resting place shall be greatly honored."[85] Indeed we can now behold the fulfillment of this prophecy. If it is new to the eye, it is already familiar to the ear, and its novelty is all the more pleasing in that it is attested by ancient authority. Enough now about the holy sepulcher.

83. 1 Cor 9:24.
84. Job 3:22.
85. Is 11:10.

CHAPTER TWELVE

BETHPAGE

WHAT SHALL I SAY OF BETHPAGE, the little priestly village which I had almost passed over, and which mystically symbolizes both confession and the priesthood? "Bethpage" indeed is translated as "the house of the mouth;"[1] and it is written, "The word is near, in your very mouth and in your heart."[2] Remember to keep the word not in one only, but in both at once. In the heart of a sinner the word effects a salutary compunction, while in his mouth it supplants harmful confusion which might impede necessary confession.

As Scripture says, "There is a shame leading to sin, and there is also a shame leading to glory."[3] The good shame leads you to be ashamed to sin or to have sinned. Even if perhaps there is no human witness, you will be all the more confounded by the searching regard of God; considering his great purity in comparison to men, as well as how he is all the more offended by the sinner because of his greater distance from all sin. If we consider a good conscience as being our glory, then certainly this sort of shame leads to glory and avoids reproach. It either eliminates sin entirely, or at least punishes by penance and removes by confession those sins which have been committed.

1. That is, the mouth of entrance of the valley, according to Jerome. Others read "house of green figs." And many other interpretations are given. See Jerome, *Liber de Nominibus Hebraicis*, PL 23:839-840.
2. Deut 30:14; Rom 10:8.
3. Sir 4:25.

But if anyone is ashamed to confess the cause of his confusion, this sort of shame leads to sin and loses the glory of a good conscience.[4] The evil which his confusion was spurring him to cast out of his heart is now unable to pass the lips which have been sealed by this misplaced shame. On the contrary, he ought to follow the example of David and say, "I have not sealed my lips, O Lord, you know it."[5]

I think David was reproaching himself for this sort of foolish and unreasonable shame when he said, "Because I was silent, my bones grew old."[6] That is why he desired that a gate should be placed before his lips and that the portal of his mouth might be open for confession, but closed to excuses.[7] Indeed he quite plainly requested this of the Lord in prayer, since he knew that confession and splendor are his works.[8] In other words, we should not remain silent concerning the splendor of his divine goodness and power, nor hide our own misery. This double confession is a great good, but it is also a gift of God.[9] Therefore he prays, "Do not incline my heart to evil words, or to making excuses for my sins."[10]

This is why priests as ministers of the Word must be solicitous to use toward erring hearts such a moderation in the administering of the word of reproach and fear as will not frighten them away from pronouncing the word of confession. Let them open hearts in such a way as not to stop mouths. But let them refuse absolution to those who repent without confessing; since indeed, the heart believes, and one is justified; the lips confess, and one is saved.[11] On the other hand, confession is as absent from the dead as if they did not exist.[12] Therefore those who have the word in their mouth but not in their heart are either deceitful or vain, while those who have it in their heart but not in their mouth are either timid or proud.

4. Ibid.
5. Ps 39:10.
6. Ps 31:3.
7. Ps 140:3-4.
8. Ps 110:3.

9. Eph 2:8.
10. Ps 140:4.
11. Rom 10:10.
12. Sir 17:26.

CHAPTER THIRTEEN

BETHANY

DRESSED AS I AM, I ought not to pass over in silence Bethany, the house of obedience.[1] This is the village of Mary and Martha, where Lazarus was raised to life.[2] Here we have the image of the two ways of life, as well as of God's wonderful mercy towards sinners[3] and of the virtue of obedience—not to mention the fruits of penance.

It will suffice here[4] to indicate briefly that neither zeal for good works[5] nor the repose of holy contemplation[6] nor the tears of penance[7] are acceptable to him except in "Bethany;" for he so esteemed obedience as to prefer it to his very life, being made obedient to his Father even unto death.[8]

These then are those riches promised in prophecy to the word of the Lord: "The Lord will console Sion," he says, "he will strengthen all her ruins, and take his delight in her wastes. He will make her deserts as the garden of the Lord. Gladness and rejoicing will be found in her, the voice of praise and thanksgiving."[9] These delights of our world, this

---

1. Bernard again follows Jerome here, *Liber de Nominibus Hebraicis*, PL 23:849-40. Others have "house of the poor," and many other derivations.
2. Jn 11:1.
3. Jn 11:38-44. Lazarus four days in the tomb is a figure of the soul in sin.
4. Bernard develops this theme at length in Asspt. See especially, serm. 3, OB 5:238-244.
5. Of which Martha is the type; see Lk 10:40-41.
6. Of which Mary is the type; see Lk 10:39, 42.
7. Of which Lazarus is the type; see Jn 11:31.
8. Phil 2:8.
9. Is 51:3.

heavenly treasure and this heritage of all believers is now entrusted to your care, beloved brothers. It is confided to your bravery and prudence. However, you will not be able to keep this heavenly trust in safety and in truth if you trust in these qualities of yours, but only if you always confide in the help of God. Know that no man prevails by his own strength,[10] and repeat therefore with the Prophet, "The Lord is my support, my refuge and my liberator,"[11] and again, "To you do I look for my strength, O God, my protector; my God whose mercy goes before me."[12] Ever say, "Not unto us O Lord, not unto us give glory, but unto your own name,"[13] so that in all things he might be blessed who teaches your hands for war and your fingers for the fight.[14]

10. 1 Sam 2:9.
11. Ps 17:3.
12. Ps 58:10-11.
13. Ps 113:9. (Ps 113b:1) This text was the official motto of the Knights Templars.
14. Ps 143:1.

SELECTED BIBLIOGRAPHY

ON GRACE AND FREE CHOICE

Critical Edition

"De gratia et libero arbitrio." Ed. J. Leclercq and H. M. Rochais. *S. Bernardi opera.* Vol. 3 (Rome: Editiones Cistercienses, 1963) pp. 165-203.

Charpentier, M. "Traité de la Grace et du Libre Arbitre" *Oeuvres complètes de Saint Bernard.* Vol. 2 (Paris: Vives, 1866) pp. 494-531.

Dies Ramos, G. "De la gracia y del libre arbitrio," *Obras completas de San Bernardo.* Vol. 2, Biblioteca de Autores Cristianos, 130 (Madrid: Editorial Catolico, 1955) pp. 931-974.

Williams, Watkin W. *The Treatise of St Bernard Concerning Grace and Free Will* (New York: Macmillan/ London: SPCK, 1920).

Studies

Bavaud, G. "Les rapports de la grâce et des libre arbitre. Un dialogue entre saint Bernard, saint Thomas d'Aquin et Calvin," *Verbum Caro,* 14 (1960) 328-338.

Châtillon, J. "Influence de saint Bernard sur le scolastique," *Saint Bernard Théologien: Actes du Congrès di Dijon, 15-19 septembre 1953.* ASOC 9 (1953) 268-288.

Danielou, J. "St Bernard et les pères grecs," Ibid., pp. 46-55.

Dimier, A. "Pour la fiche *spiritus libertatis,*" *Revue du moyen âge latin* 3 (1947) 56-60.

Faust, V. "Bernhards 'Liber de Gratia et Libero Arbitrio': Bedeutung, Quellen und Einfluss," *Analecta Monastica* 6. Studia Anselmiana, 50 (Rome, 1962), 35-52.

Forest, A. "Das Erlebnis des *Consensus Voluntatis* beim heiligen Bernhard," *Bernhard von Clairvaux, Mönch und Mystiker* (Wiesbaden 1955), pp. 120-127.

Gilson, E. *The Spirit of Medieval Philosophy* (New York, 1940).

Gilson, E. *The Mystical Theology of Saint Bernard* (New York, 1940).

Hiss, W. *Die Anthropologie Bernhards von Clairvaux* (Berlin, 1964).

Javelet, R. *Image et ressemblance au douzième siècle.* 2 vols. (Paris, 1967) 1:189-197.

Kleineidam, E. "De triplici libertate. Anselm von Laon oder Bernhard von Clairvaux? " *Cîteaux* 11 (1960) 56-62.

Lottin, O. "Libre arbitre et liberté depuis saint Anselme jusqu'à la fin du XIIIᵉ siècle," *Psychologie et moral au XIIᵉ et XIIIᵉ siècles.* 6 vols. (Louvain Gembloux, Mont César, 1942-1960) 1:11-224.

Otto, S. *Die Funktion des Bildbegriffes in der Theologie des 12 Jahrhunderts.* Beiträge zur Geschichte der Philosophie und Theologie des Mittelalters 40:1 (Münster, 1963).

Sartori, L. "Natura e Grazia nella Dottrina di San Bernardo," *Studia Patavina,* 1 (1954) 41-64.

Schaffner, O. "Die 'nobilis Deo creatura' des heiligen Bernhard von Clairvaux," *Geist und Leben,* 23 (1950) 43-57.

Standaert, Maur. "La doctrine de l'image chez saint Bernard," *Ephemerides Theologicae Lovaniensis,* 23 (1947) 70-129. Also in *In Sylloge Excerptorum e Dissertationibus* 14-4 (Louvain, 1947).

——. "Le principe de l'ordination dans la théologie spirituelle de saint Bernard," *Collectanea OCR* 8 (1946) 178-216.

Venuta, G. *Libero Arbitrio e Libertà della Grazia nel Pensiero di S. Bernardo.* (Rome: Ferrari, 1953).

Von Ivánka, E. "La structure de l'âme selon saint Bernard." *Saint Bernard Théologien,* pp. 202-208.

IN PRAISE OF THE NEW KNIGHTHOOD

Critical Edition

"Liber ad Milites Templi: de laude novae militiae." Ed. J. Leclercq and H. M. Rochais. *S. Bernardi opera.* Vol. 3 (Rome: Editiones Cistercienses, 1963) pp. 312-239.

Translations

Charpentier, M. "Louange de la nouvelle milice des templiers." *Oeuvres complètes de saint Bernard.* Vol. 2 (Paris: Vives, 1866), pp. 388-412.

De Solms, E. "A la louange de la milice nouvelle." *St. Bernard* (Namur: Soleil Levant, 1958) pp. 152-191.

Diez Ramos, G. "De la excelencia de la Nueva Milicia," *Obras completas de San Bernardo.* Vol. 2, Biblioteca de Autores Cristianos 130 (Madrid: Editorial Catolica, 1955) pp. 853-881.

Studies

Carrière, V. "Les débuts de l'Ordre du Temple en France," *Le Moyen Age,* 18 (1914) 308-334.

Cartulaire général de l'Ordre du Temple. Ed. Marquis d'Albon. 2 vols. (Paris, 1913). Note especially, *Regula commilitonum Christi,* ed. G. Schnürer, 1:129-153.

Charrier, H. "Les sens militaire chez saint Bernard," *Saint Bernard et son temps.* 2 vols. (Dijon, 1929) 1:68-74.

Commission d'Histoire de l'Ordre de Cîteaux. *Bernard de Clairvaux* (Paris: Alsatia, 1953). See especially the *Table analytique* V, 6, pp. 673-674.

Cousin, P. "Les débuts de l'ordre des Templiers et saint Bernard," *Mélange saint Bernard* (Dijon: Trouve, 1953) pp. 41-52.

De Curzon, H., ed. *La Règle du Temple* (Paris, 1886).

Delaruelle, E. "L'Idée de crusade chez saint Bernard," *Mélange saint Bernard.* Pp. 53-67.

De Poorter, A. "Le texte original de la Règle du Templiers," *Annual de la Societé d'Emulation de Bruges,* 62 (1912) 193-198.

Dessubré, M. *Bibligraphie de l'ordre des Templiers* (Paris, 1928).

Hugh (of Payens [?], of St Victor [more probable]). *Epistola.* Ed. Jean Leclercq. *Recueil d'études sur saint Bernard et ses écrits.* Vol. 2 (Rome, 1966) pp. 93-96.

Leclercq, Jean. "Un document sur les débuts des Templiers." *Recueil,* pp. 87-100.

Léonard, M. *Introduction au Cartulaire manuscrit del'Ordre du Temple* (Paris, 1930).

Lobet, M. *L'histoire mystérieuse et tragique des Templiers* (Liège, 1944).

Luddy, Ailbe J. *Life and Teaching of Saint Bernard* (Dublin: Gill, 1950). See especially, pp. 172-178.

Melville, M. *La vie des Templiers* (Gallimard, 1951).

Oliver, A. "El 'Libre del Ordre de Cavalleria' de Ramon Llull y et 'De laude Novae Militia' de s. Bernard," *Estudios Llulianos,* 8 (1958) 175-186.

Pensoye, P. "Saint Bernard et la règle du Temple." *Études Traditionnelles,* 364 (1961) 81-88.

Prawer, Joshua. *Histoire du royaume latin de Jérusalem* (Paris, 1969).

Rousset, P. "Les origines et la caractère de la Deuzième Croisade, Saint Bernard et la Croisade." *Saint Bernard et son temps.* 1:152-168.

Schnürer, G. *Die Ursprüngliche Templerregel* (Freiburg-im-Breisgau, 1903).

——. "Zur ersten Organization der Templer," *Historisches Jahrbuch,* 32 (1911) 298-314.

Sclafert, C. "Lettre inédite de Hugues de Saint-Victor aux Chevaliers du Temple," *Revue d'ascétique et de mystique,* 34 (1958) 275-299.

Seward, Desmond. "Dissolution of the Templars," *History Today,* 31 (1971) 628-635.

William of Tyr. *Historia rerum transmarinarum.* Liber 21, c. 7. PL 201:526-527.

Williams, E. "Cîteaux et la seconde croisade." *Revue d'histoire ecclesiastique,* 49 (1954) 116-151.

INDEX

On Grace and Free Choice
(Numerals refer to paragraph numbers)

Adam
  12, 20, 21, 29
Appetite, natural
  2, 3, 5, 41
Book of life
  44
  (see also *Salvation*)
Choice
  defined: 11; *passim*
  (see also *Free choice*)
Christ
  7, 26, 36-40, 49, 50
  Jesus 1
  Son of God 32
Compulsion
  40
Consent, voluntary
  2-6, 9, 36, 38, 40, 41, 44-6,
  49
Consummation
  49
Contemplation
  15
Conversion
  19
Counsel, free
  11, 24, 26
  (see also *Freedom of Counsel*)
Creation
  49

Death
  7, 13, 21, 26, 37
Devil
  9, 18, 22, 29, 35, 45
  Fallen angels 35
Fasting
  49
Fear
  17
Fear of God
  16
Free choice
  Pro, 2, 4, 6, 7, 11, 12, 15, 18,
  19, 20, 24, 26-8, 31, 33-5,
  41, 42, 46-9
  (see also *Freedom of choice*)
Freedom
  1, 5, 6, 24, 25, 36, *et passim*
  of the will, 4, 39, 49
  (see also *Will*)
  spirit of, 49
Freedom from necessity = free-
  of life or glory
  6, 7, 9, 12
Freedom from sin = freedom of
  nature = freedom of counsel
  6-8, 10-12, 15, 20, 21, 26,
  27, 30, 31, 34, 36
Freedom from sorrow = freedom of grace = freedom of

pleasure
6-8, 11, 13, 15, 20, 21, 24,
26, 27, 30, 31
Freedom of choice
15, 16, 18, 19, 21, 22, 24,
28, 30, 41
(see also *Free choice*)
Good Work
49
Grace
Pro, 1, 2, 4, 9, 12, 17, 18,
28, 33, 42, 44, 48, 49
Guilt
37
Happiness
15, 51
Image of God
27, 28, 30-35, 41
Joy
49
False joy 14
Justification
48
Likeness of God
28-30, 32, 34
Love
16, 17, 38, 51
Charity 29
Inordinate, 17
Memory
49
Merit(s)
43, 45, 46, 48-50
Nature
18
Necessity
5, 10, 24, 36, 47
Pilgrim
43
Pleasure
11, 13, 14
(see also *Freedom from sorrow*)

Power
19, 20, 24, 26, 28
Power of God
26, 29
Punishment
45
Rational creature
4, 30
Reason
3, 4, 15
Reformation
49
Resurrection
35
Salvation
2, 36, 41-4, 48
cup of, 48
eternal life, 43
Self-love
38
Sense perception
3, 4, 5
Sin
9, 21, 48
Original, 42
Sorrow
13, 21, 24, 28, 29, 36
Spirit, divine
1, 35, 41, 50
Suffering(s)
8, 9, 14, 31
Virtue(s)
13, 17, 43
Will (human)
1, 3-6, 9-11, 17, 18, 23, 24,
31, 35-41, 45, 46, 48, 50, 51
Freedom of, 18
Weakness of, 38
Will of God
12, 19
Wisdom
Pro, 19, 20, 24, 26, 28-34, 49

In Praise of the New Knighthood
(Numerals refer to page numbers)

Absolution
165
Adam
149, 158, 159
Armor
133
Atonement
153
Bethany
166
Bethlehem
146, 148
Bethpage
164
Body
130, 131, 155, 162
Bravery
140, 167
Chess
139
Christ
130, 131, 134, 138, 139,
144, 146, 147, 152, 154,
156, 158-61
Baptism of, 152
Death of, 154, 162
Divinity, 157
Humanity, 157
Bread of angels 146
Infant God 148

Justice 161
King 134, 143
Living Bread 146
Lord of armies 137
Savior 144
True Solomon 141
Wisdom of God 153, 161
Word 146, 149
Compunction
164
Concupiscence
159
Confession
164, 165
Conscience
133, 164, 165
Contemplation
166
Conversion
144
Death
130-32, 134, 154, 155, 157,
158, 160-62, 166
Law of, 162
Rights of, 160
Debt
to death, 160
to sin, 156-57
Discipline
138

Faith
130, 135, 160
Falconry
139
Flesh
129, 146, 149, 150, 156-9
Hair
139
Happiness
154
Humility
151
Jerusalem
135-7, 142, 143, (144-145)
Jew(s)
148, 149
Jordan
152
Josaphat, valley of
150
Judgment
150, 151
Justice
135, 156-61
Justification
157
Knighthood
129, 130, 132, 137
Love
143, 159
Martyr(s)
130, 145
Mercy
151, 157, 162
Miracles
156, 160
Monk(s)
129, 140
Mount Calvary
153
Mount of Olives
150
Nazareth
148

Obedience
138, 143, 158, 166
Pagan(s)
134, 135, 143
Penance
164, 166
Pilgrim(s)
162
Poverty
137, (139), 143, (160-1)
Pride
131, 136
Priest(hood)
164, 165
Reason
155
Redemption
162
Salvation
160
Sepulcher, Holy
154, 162, 163
Sion
135, 136, 144
Sin(s)
138, 155, 156, 158-62, 154
Remission of, 154
Soul
130, 131, 155
Sword
132, 134, 135, 141, 142
The two swords, 130, 135
Trinity
152
Troubadours
139
Virtue(s)
142, 145
War
134, 140, 167
Works, good
166

CISTERCIAN PUBLICATIONS

Titles Listing

1977

THE CISTERCIAN FATHERS SERIES

THE WORKS OF BERNARD OF CLAIRVAUX

Treatises I (*Apologia* to Abbot William, On Precept and Dispensation) CF 1

On the Song of Songs I CF 4

On the Song of Songs II CF 7

Treatises II (The Steps of Humility, On Loving God) CF 13

Five Books on Consideration CF 37

THE WORKS OF WILLIAM OF ST THIERRY

On Contemplating God, Prayer, Meditations CF 3

Exposition on the Song of Songs CF 6

The Enigma of Faith CF 9

The Golden Epistle CF 12

THE WORKS OF AELRED OF RIEVAULX

Treatises I (On Jesus at the Age of Twelve, Rule for a Recluse, The Pastoral Prayer) CF 2

Spiritual Friendship CF 5

THE WORKS OF GUERRIC OF IGNY

Liturgical Sermons
two volumes CF 8, CF 32

OTHER WRITERS

The Letters of Adam of Perseigne CF 21

The Way of Love CF 16

John of Ford, Sermons on The Song of Songs CF 29

THE CISTERCIAN STUDIES SERIES

CISTERCIAN STUDIES

The Cistercian Spirit: A Symposium in Memory of Thomas Merton CS 3

The Eleventh-century Background of Citeaux by Bede Lackner CS 8

Studies in Medieval Cistercian History, edited Joseph F. O'Callahan CS 13

Contemplative Community edited M. Basil Pennington CS 21

Bernard of Clairvaux: Studies Presented to Dom Jean Leclercq CS 23

William of St Thierry: The Man and His Work by J. M. Dechanet CS 10

Thomas Merton: The Man and His Work by Dennis Q. McInerny CS 27

Cistercian Sign Language by Robert Barakat CS 11

Studies in Medieval Cistercian History, II ed. John R. Sommerfeldt CS 24

Bernard of Clairvaux and the Cistercian Spirit by Jean Leclercq CS 16

MONASTIC TEXTS AND STUDIES

The Climate of Monastic Prayer by Thomas Merton CS 1

Evagrius Ponticus: Praktikos and Chapters on Prayer CS 4

The Abbot in Monastic Tradition by Pierre Salmon CS 14

Why Monks? by Francois Vandenbroucke CS 17

Silence: Silence in the Rule of St Benedict by Ambrose Wathen CS 22

The Sayings of the Desert Fathers tr Benedicta Ward CS 59

One Yet Two: Monastic Tradition East and West CS 29

The Spirituality of Western Christendom ed. E. R. Elder CS 30

Russian Mystics by Sergius Bolshakoff CS 26

In Quest of The Absolute by Joseph Weber CS 51